Science and the Sons of Genius
Studies on Humphry Davy
Edited by Sophie Forgan

Science and the Sons of Genius:
Studies on Humphry Davy

Papers presented at the Royal Institution, London,
at the Davy Bicentenary Symposium
with an Introduction by Sophie Forgan

Copyright: the authors
typing by Joan Wilkins Associates Ltd.

Front cover: Humphry Davy, after the
portrait by Lawrence, reproduced by
kind permission of the Royal Institution.

ISBN 0-905927-55-9
Published by Science Reviews Ltd.
3/4 St. Andrew's Hill
London EC4V 5BY
England
1980

Contents

Preface and Acknowledgements - Frank Greenaway   ii

Contributors   iii

List of Abbreviations   v

Introduction
    Sophie Forgan   vii

1. The Young Humphry Davy: or John Tonkin's Lament   1
    Michael Neve

2. Humphry Davy, 'The Sons of Genius', and the Idea of Glory   33
    Trevor H. Levere

3. Humphry Davy, Reformer   59
    J.Z. Fullmer

4. Davy and Gay-Lussac: Competition and Contrast   95
    Maurice Crosland

5. Davy's Chemical Outlook: The Acid Test   121
    John Hedley Brooke

6. Davy's 'Intellectual Delight' and his Lectures at the Royal Institution   177
    Robert Siegfried

7. Davy's Salmonia   201
    David Knight

A Note on Humphry Davy's Experiments on the Respiration of Nitrous Oxide and Other Gases   231
    E.B. Smith

Postscript - Song   239

Index   241

PREFACE AND ACKNOWLEDGEMENTS

These essays were presented at a symposium which celebrated the bicentenary of the birth on 17th December 1778 of Humphry Davy.

Davy was associated for the greater part of his scientific life with the Royal Institution of Great Britain, an organisation which flourishes today with vigour, one of the sources of which may be attributed to Davy's genius. The papers were therefore very properly read at the Royal Institution, where the participants met and were entertained by a reading of Davy's own verse in the library which he used. Other receptions were held by the Science Museum and by the Chemical Society, organisations which did not exist in his day, but which he would have applauded were he alive today.

The Royal Institution was the principal host for the occasion, but official sponsorship was also accorded by the International Union of the History and Philosophy of Science. Generous financial support and hospitality was also provided by:

    The Central Electricity Generating Board
    Imperial Chemical Industries Ltd.
    John Harvey & Sons Ltd., Bristol
    The National Coal Board
    The Royal Society
    Shell International Chemical Company Ltd.

Some of the work reported during the symposium also benefitted from the basic resource of the Leverhulme Trust grant for research on the history of the Royal Institution. Thanks for advice on the programme are due to the officers of The British Society for the History of Science, The Society for the History of Alchemy and Chemistry, and the Historical Group of the Chemical Society. Finally, the symposium could not have developed into such a successful gathering of colleagues and friends without the able work of the Executive Secretary, Mrs.Phyllida Lindsay, and the enthusiastic support of the Royal Institution.

                                          Frank Greenaway
                                          Chairman of the
                                              Organising Committee.

CONTRIBUTORS

Michael Neve
    University College, London.

Trevor H. Levere
    Institute for the History and Philosophy of
    Science and Technology, University of Toronto,
    Toronto M5S 1A1, Canada.

J.Z. Fullmer
    Department of History, Ohio State University,
    Columbus, Ohio.

Maurice Crosland
    Unit for the History of Science, University of
    Kent, Canterbury.

John Hedley Brooke
    Department of History, University of Lancaster.

Robert Siegfried
    History of Science Department, University of
    Wisconsin, Madison.

David Knight
    Department of Philosophy, University of Durham.

E.B. Smith
    Physical Chemistry Laboratory, Oxford.

Sophie Forgan
    Teesside Polytechnic, Middlesbrough, Cleveland.

List of Abbreviations

<u>Memoirs</u>   John Davy, <u>Memoirs of the Life of Sir Humphry Davy, Bart.</u>, 2 vols., London, 1836.

<u>Works</u>   John Davy (ed.), <u>The Collected Works of Sir Humphry Davy, Bart.</u>, 9 vols., London, 1839-1840.

<u>Fragmentary Remains</u>   John Davy (ed.), <u>Fragmentary Remains, Literary and Scientific of Sir Humphry Davy, Bart.</u>, London, 1858.

Paris, <u>Life</u>   J.A. Paris, <u>The Life of Sir Humphry Davy, Bart.</u>, 2 vols., London, 1831.

R.I. Davy Ms   Davy Manuscripts in the Archives of the Royal Institution, London.

<u>D.N.B.</u>   <u>Dictionary of National Biography</u>.

Introduction

Sophie Forgan

Humphry Davy has been described by many names: the mercurial chemist, romantic genius, poet and philosopher, the 'Pilot' of Penzance, to name but a few. There are others less attractive, intellect-ual entrepreneur, snob and social climber. Such a plethora of contradictory epithets indicates first of all how controversial a figure Davy was. To historians he remains a controversial subject. There is indeed no full-scale biography of Davy which has withstood the test of time and critical examination. A number of excellent studies exist, but Davy has so far eluded extended treatment. The essays printed here do not attempt to fill that place, but rather to explore certain areas and certain problems. Three principal themes may be identified which surface repeatedly in the papers.

First of all there is a preoccupation with the 'fragmentary' quality of Davy's life, pinpointed so early by Berzelius. Our view of Davy has long been set by Berzelius' percipient phrase, and accounts of Davy's successes are so often balanced against his 'failures', his failure to advance chemistry by 'a full century', his tantalizing nearness to achieving a unitary theory of compounds, his habit of leaving only tentative suggestions rather than expounding comprehensive theories. This question is approached from several angles. Michael Neve suggests that the fragmentary, undirected aspect of Davy's life may owe something to his ambivalent attitude towards medicine, and brings evidence to show that until as late as 1807 Davy might yet have opted for a medical career, as did his brother John. His involvement with Beddoes' Pneumatic Institution however ensured that he received no recognised medical training, and in the event of course nothing came of it. Neve's study of Davy's Cornish background reveals not only the familiar Romantic element, but also how heavily directed the society Davy left was towards medicine.

On the other hand Trevor Levere asserts that there was an underlying unity which bound together the Romantic youthful Davy with the successful scientist who worked on such useful projects as the safety lamp. These were not unconnected fragments in an unfocussed life. If one looks at Davy's idea of glory, the distinction between the romantic and utilitarian may be eliminated. In scientific discovery, glory was married to utility, for material benefits were conferred upon mankind, while the sublime speculations of science delighted the intellect in a manner far superior to poetry, for poetry had in itself no absolute utility. Certainly Davy's move to the Royal Institution marked a transition from predominantly Romantic to more utilitarian concerns. There was however no necessary contradiction between the two, but rather a mutual reinforcement. June Fullmer also sees Davy's life as one bound together by a unifying purpose, by a single-minded devotion to reform. Davy's years as President of the Royal Society are scrutinised and reveal considerable achievements, which have however been obscured by the more dramatic struggles of the years following his death.

The second theme concerns Davy's place in the history of chemistry. On the one hand, the crucial importance of the French tradition is reiterated, that much of Davy's work should be seen in the context of rivalry between France and England. As June Fullmer insists, it was Davy's aim to reform the conceptual foundations of chemistry in order to destroy the errors of Lavoisier's theories. Davy regarded the French contributions to chemistry more in the nature of obstacles diverting chemistry from its true path, which was one stemming from essentially Newtonian traditions. Maurice Crosland again emphasizes the intellectual rivalry between France and England, personified in the competition of Davy and Gay-Lussac. Differences of chemical style, professional background and personality accentuated the contrast, summed up by Crosland as the contrast between classical and romantic.

On the other hand, J.H. Brooke examines the view of Davy as a reformer of Lavoisier's theory of acids, and suggests certain important qualifications which need to be made to this interpretation. He then reveals a situation suffused with irony, for rather than supplying a hydrogen theory of acids to replace Lavoisier's oxygen theory, the particular ontology Davy held at that time made it impossible for him even to countenance a hydrogen theory. Furthermore, Davy's contemporaries wrongly credited him with a theory which is usually supposed to be right, and did this only to show that it was wrong. Brooke shows how far Davy was misrepresented even by those who acknowledged their debt to him.

A third theme concerns the role of science as purveyor of intellectual delights generally regarded as the preserve of the visual and literary arts, and brings the wheel full circle back to the Romantic element in Davy's philosophy. Robert Siegfried suggests that the roots of Davy's creativity lay in his delight in his 'intellectual being'. Science presented an intellectual challenge and delight in understanding, that no other vocation could provide. Brooke too refers to Davy's attitude to chemical hypotheses, the 'secret amusements of the mind', as a game of chess unrivalled by any similar mental activity, never more so than when there were French theories to be torn down. Levere shows how the admiration of scientific genius by the Romantic poets was not reciprocated by their idol. To Davy it was only the scientific, not the poetic genius, who could on 'wings sublime to soar'. Finally, we meet in David Knight's paper, the sage at leisure and the ageing philosopher who hoped to encourage younger spirits to soar and surpass his achievements, as in his own poem the parent eagles taught their young to fly upwards into the sun.

Naturally, there are many problems and aspects of Davy's life and career which were ignored. There is for example little about his work in agricultural chemistry, on the safety lamp, or about his relationship to the changing fortunes of the Royal Institution. The symposium rather highlighted the many contradictions to which there is as yet no conclusive answer. The most obvious of these is in Davy's character. Was he the snob and social climber he was so often alleged to be? The evidence of Berzelius says yes, that of June Fullmer denies it; for he was also the man who tried to open up the Royal Society to those of merit from all classes. Was his social climbing a desire to move among the elite of intellect rather than simply the elite of class? His well-known dislike of the wealthy bourgeois, an attitude indeed so typical of the country gentleman, was reinforced by what he regarded as their 'unintellectual' profiteering attitude towards science. Was he 'malleable' as Morris Berman suggests in <u>Social Change and Scientific Organization</u> (1978), or did he need little pushing from the governors of the Royal Institution? We know indeed very little about his specific intentions concerning research when he joined the Institution. We also know that he was already a good and unusual geologist. It may therefore be a distortion to see his geological work simply as a constraint preventing him from doing 'more important' work in chemistry. Was this and other work at the Royal Institution a distraction leaving him no time to create a comprehensive theoretical structure for chemistry, or was the situation in chemistry intellectually far more complex, and furthermore, Davy a scientist whose main achievements arose out of his efforts to destroy what he saw as pernicious French theories? Yet he received honours and recognition in France, and was as much at home on the Continent as in England. Despite his patriotic love for England, his journeys to the Continent became, as Neve comments, increasingly a retreat from London. As Knight too points out, it is in his rootlessness that Davy seems especially 'modern'.

Centenaries and bicentenaries provide welcome occasions for celebrating the achievements of great men. The essays printed here however are no mere laudatory biography. Historians are now all too conscious that history written in terms of the lives of great men creates a false perspective, and indeed, by overpraising may perversely fail to do justice to the interest and complexity of the individual subject. In Davy's career there is ambiguity and ambivalence in plenty. An analysis adds much both to our knowledge of Davy and to our understanding of the development of science in late Georgian England.

The Young Humphry Davy: or John Tonkin's Lament
Michael Neve

No scientific career, let alone one launched in the difficult waters of the early nineteenth century, can be altogether free of failures and successes, of smooth and choppy passages. It is a feature of much writing in the history of science to skim over the periods of routine and lack of glamour in the lives of those (usually celebrated) figures that it elects for historical illumination. Too often, a smooth trajectory is presented, of an easy flight from obscurity to celebrity, from ignorance to genius. It is still striking how questions normally asked of other historical figures, questions of power, of plagiarism, of prejudice and strategy, how these continue to be ignored when the lives of scientists are examined. Occasionally, as with the geologist Sir Charles Lyell, it is even considered an insult to assume that a historical view of an individual's place in the history of a science is not necessarily identical with that same individual's assessment of the question. There continues to be a danger that one historiography exists for all those not engaged in natural philosophy, and another for those who do.[1]

Part of the greatness of Sir Humphry Davy lies in his awareness that no career is free from self-doubt and a sense of fractured hopes, for all that is known of Davy's love of social glamour and international success. This is part of the reason why <u>Consolations in Travel</u> (1830) is one of the great documents of European philosophy in the early nineteenth century. That work argues various philosophical propositions, but is also an attempt on the part of its author to bring together and organise the lost strains of a Romantic consciousness that had, in the course of his career, been disconnected and diffused. There is, as many writers have noted, a curious link between the beginning and the end of Davy's career, connected as they are by this commitment to establishing a Romanticist view of life, one that brought together the different talents that had each in its turn, been singled out and dispersed as the ardent young poet and medical apprentice had become the celebrated metropolitan scientist. Davy's career is full of fascinating little asides, sometimes leading nowhere in particular, which nonetheless offer insights into the man's personality.

The early years are striking, but so too is Davy's end, an end that rivals Keats, whose genius

Davy resembles, and one that occurs in a Europe that had for Davy become a personal retreat. The fishing expeditions to Austria, the sojourn in the flat marshlands of Ravenna, and of course the extraordinary journey from Rome to Geneva. There is even a hint in <u>Consolations in Travel</u> that Davy came close to an affiliation with Roman Catholicism in his last moments. Many other aspects of his life attract attention: his ideas on genius; his general views on science, which he sees as both generated by class society and yet as assisting in holding that same society together; and of course his marriage. How extraordinarily little is really heard in the history of science of the <u>wives</u> of scientists let alone their marriages! Yet that formidable socialite Jane Apreece (1780-1855) claims her place in the <u>D.N.B.</u>, being 'best known as the wife of Sir Humphry Davy'. She certainly warrants considerable examination. Davy also had an interesting distrust of the city, as a new historical phenomenon, and makes some related and striking remarks on the nearest non-metropolitan society to his own that retained a peasantry in its social structure - Ireland. His observations on Ireland are unusual, since they reflect his scientific and his political thinking. He noted, conventionally, both its backwardness and ignorance. There is that hilarious letter from the 1805 journey, from Limerick:

> The great vice of the people is want
> of perseverance: nothing is finished:
> they begin grandly and magnificently,
> but complete very little. In mining,
> they build machinery before they have
> discovered a vein; in the fisheries,
> they erect their cellars before they
> have purchased nets; and they build
> magnificent stables, which they intend
> for their studs, but which they are
> themselves obliged to inhabit.
> Foresight and prudence are unknown.[2]

But Davy also suggests that if the power of urban middlemen could be removed, then a progressive agrarian society might appear, administered by a benign landed ruling class. He also tells an anecdote of administering physic to a young boy, and of giving him money, and notes 'it is only in the towns that the lower classes are depraved'. Davy was strikingly well paid for the lectures that he gave in Dublin, in 1811 especially, and it may well be that it was Ireland that was best suited to his message of the uses of chemistry in agriculture, a message that he had also propagated the English landed classes. Certainly too, Davy was never free from that great Celtic legacy, superstition. He wrote, towards the end of his life, and in Würzen of all places, a strange Irish short story,

'The Last of the O'Donoghues', with its vision of a pre-Christian Europe, and an Ireland before the arrival of St. Patrick. Even the heavy fraternal solidarity of his brother's biography cannot conceal the fears and forebodings that beset the dying Celt in the Protestant stronghold of Geneva. The following paragraph should be read bearing in mind the young Davy's work and speculations on physiological irritability and the materiality of thought; and his lifelong anti-materialism.[3]

> He had a dread of a <u>post mortem</u> examination, founded on an idea which occurred to his active mind, that it was possible for sensation to remain in the animal fibre after the loss of irritability and the power of giving proof to others of its existence. Consequently, such an investigation not having been made, his disease, as to its exact kind and the immediate cause of his death, must ever remain doubtful.
>
> Before I quit this painful subject, I should remark that he had also a horror of being buried alive, before animation was completely extinct, and he desired that the interment should not be performed till after ten days. I was very anxious

> to have complied with this injunction, merely because it was his request; but at Geneva it was impossible, being contrary to law to keep a body so long unburied. The keeping it even three days was an indulgence; and as signs of putrefaction then began to appear, I made no opposition to the performance of the ceremony.[4]

In terms of his own ideas of life, Humphry Davy was indeed buried alive.

Davy's career has then, its fascinating minor asides, as well as a consistent theme of a Romantic philosopher attempting to weld together the elements of a brilliant but unfocussed life. The Cornwall of his youth retained its pull on his poetic imagination, as we know. But are there any other links between his early and later life that tie in with this general pattern, and which in turn reflect on the sense of incompleteness that Davy's life suggests?

My feeling is that one small item of interest does exist in this connection, and that is Davy's unfinished and eccentric relationship with the practice of medicine. I do not put forward Davy's medical 'non-career' as any great missing link in the chain of his being. But - at least up to 1807 -

Davy does not seem to have completely relinquished the possibility of establishing himself as a doctor, and I hope that this marginal aspect of his career may prove of interest.

I take as my starting point a portrait of Davy, one whose provenance and purpose seems always to have been a little mysterious. It hangs in Jesus College, Cambridge, where Davy registered as a Fellow Commoner on July 3rd, 1804, apparently with the purpose of gaining some kind of medical degree. It seems that he may have been on his way to Scotland, to geologise. John Davy gives us a perfectly straightforward explanation for this move, suggesting that 'he was probably induced to form this plan by a prospect of fortune, in a professional career, infinitely greater than he had any right to expect from the mere prosecution of science.'[5] Nonetheless, Humphry was doing extremely well at the Royal Institution, speaking to very large audiences, and it is also interesting that John gives the reader the news of Humphry's thinking about medicine at an odd place in his biography i.e. not where it belongs, in 1804/1805, but well after the listing of the great work on alkalis and acids from 1807 onwards. Clearly John regarded the manoeuvre of little real importance, and he may have been right.

However the relationship to medicine is, in Davy's case, of considerable interest. He was an apprentice to that profession while at Penzance;

he became involved with one of the few medical radicals of his lifetime while at the Pneumatic Institution in Bristol, and he appears, however perfunctorily, to have considered getting back into the field, before the 1807 experiments were finalised, and before of course, the dangerous and somewhat mysterious nervous illness that came towards the end of that year. I hope to throw some glances at this missing 'non-career', in part to bring attention to some of the genuinely medical figures who helped Davy on his way, some of whom it may be said he left behind. I am thinking here of John Bingham Borlase, (1752-1813), who was mayor of the town of Penzance, a physician there who had completed his medical studies under the celebrated physician and chemistry lecturer George Fordyce (1736-1802); of Thomas Beddoes (1760-1808), a genuinely idiosyncratic medical figure, who attempted to launch a medical programme that sought to resolve the professional and technical impasse that eighteenth century medicine had come to; and of the Swiss emigré John King (1766-1846), Davy's Bristol companion, who remained tied to that city to the end of his life. These men were teachers and companions of Davy, and, along with the rather uncelebrated members of the medical faculty at Cambridge in 1804/5, in particular Busick Harwood (1745?-1814), Downing Professor of Medicine, they form the main part of my account. Alongside them are certain other medical figures, whose careers also shed a little angled light on Davy's own: Henry Penneck M.D. (1762-1834), surgeon and mayor of Penzance, whose sister was married to J.B. Borlase; John Ayrton Paris (1785-1856), who left Cambridge with considerable knowledge of mineralogy before graduating there in medicine, after a time in Edinburgh; and finally Davy's brother John (1790-1868), who made a successful career in medicine overseas, and upon whose skills and support Humphry came to rely heavily.

I have made no mention in this list of two very influential figures in Davy's early life, namely Robert Dunkin and John Tonkin (1719-1801). Tonkin was a surgeon, apothecary, five times mayor of Penzance, and Davy's guardian. I searched for clues regarding Tonkin and his career and could find none. We are therefore left with the stories that have come down to us through the biographies, the most salient features of which are the apparently quite fierce feelings that Tonkin had at the thought of his protégé heading off to Bristol to make his way in the fast lane of life, instead of remaining in a local and manageable world and settling down there to a medical career. By looking at Davy from the point of view of his medical background and semi-ambitions, I may be said to be taking up Tonkin's refrain.

It is perhaps worth mentioning that the

interesting Victorian social observer and joint editor of <u>Punch</u>, Henry Mayhew (1812-1887), was <u>not</u> put off by the absence of historical information about Tonkin and Davy, and in his little didactic book on Davy, <u>The Wonders of Science or Young Humphry Davy</u>, (London, 1860), gives us a glowing fictional version of the relationship. Davy is seen being introduced to the wonders of nature by the ageing Tonkin, who appears in a chapter entitled 'The Widowed and the Fatherless', to guide Davy into the path of genius. We see Davy learn (in a rather odd order) the secrets of HEAT, LIGHT, PHOTOGRAPHY, ELECTRICITY, only to run up against a Victorian version of parental disapproval when Tonkin hears the news of the young man's departure:

> The old gentleman however could not be made to listen to the project, and did not hesitate to denounce Humphry's drive for worldly honour as 'the wild goose-chase' which led many an ambitious simpleton astray, saying that if the boy could make up his mind to settle in his native place, he might be assured of a comfortable independence, for he would find but few able to compete with him there.[6]

Nonetheless, Humphry left Penzance. We shall go

back to Penzance later on, to see what kind of
Penzance he had left, for it was in the years of his
prime at the Royal Institution that the kind of
organized, provincial culture that Tonkin hoped to
promote actually began to appear. This pattern of
local scientific and medical developments which
began to take hold in the early years of the nineteenth century, is now being mapped out by historians of science,[7] and at least as regards his
native town, Davy was a non-contributor.[8] By
examining it in some detail, we can take up Tonkin's
theme and survey its historical outcome.

First of all, however, we must look at Bristol.
In a sense, Davy was not going to Bristol at all,
but rather to its most elegant suburb, Clifton, to
involve himself in the idiosyncratic medical programme launched by the chemist, geologist and
doctor, Thomas Beddoes. Beddoes in turn was linked
with that celebrated group of Midlands industrialists
and manufacturers that had gathered together round
the Lunar Society of Birmingham in the 1770s, among
whose members were Matthew Boulton and James Watt.
Orchestrating and recommending Davy for the position
was of course Davies Giddy or Gilbert (1767-1839),
who himself became an influential Parliamentarian,
chiefly serving the lobby interested in currency reform and agricultural protection. There was a chain
of influence that linked Cornwall to Bristol and
thence to the Midlands, a chain that was solidified

by visits and mutual interests. In terms of visits, we can think of the geological expeditions to Cornwall of Beddoes himself and of James Watt's son Gregory, and in terms of interests, we should certainly remember the great investment that Boulton and Watt had in maintaining a monopoly on the uses of a patented steam engine in smelting.[9] This produced quite fierce struggles in Cornwall itself, including a riot against Boulton and Watt's agency in 1795 and competition with those engineers, such as Jonathan Carter Hornblower (1753-1815), who attempted to rival Watt's separate condenser system. The various letters of the Giddy, Watt and Davy archives make clear this connection, from the wild culture of Cornwall, with its coastal wreckers and heavy Methodist religious culture, through the idiosyncratic medicine of Beddoes in Clifton, to the provincial grandeur of Midlands wealth, embodied in the Boulton and the Wedgwood families.

Not only was Davy simply moving along this line of influence. He was also temporarily caught up in a particularly striking and original medical experiment which sought to break a real impasse in eighteenth century medicine, both institutionally and theoretically. Despite all that has already been said about it, Thomas Beddoes' medical approach remains of interest, and it is worth setting out its background in some detail. Not the least reason for doing so is to highlight the genuine originality and indeed courage that Davy displayed when he argued against the medical theories of the eminent American medical writer Samuel Latham Mitchill (1764-1831). It was, after all, the desire to challenge Mitchill's ideas on contagion and the role of gases in the spreading of contagion that had brought Davy to Beddoes' attention in 1798. What is sometimes not stressed enough is that Davy was here involved in a <u>medical</u> and not simply a <u>chemical</u> debate.

Thomas Beddoes had good reason for both knowing Samuel Latham Mitchill, and for corresponding with him. Both men were educated in medicine at Edinburgh; both were interested in the various debates in chemistry that revolved around Priestley and Lavoisier, and importantly, both men were interested in the medical theories of the infamous John Brown (1735-1788). Brown's place in the history of eighteenth century medicine has yet to be fully explored, but studies by Günter Risse and others show its impact - on the Continent especially - to have been considerable. Brown was originally a student and intimate of the great Edinburgh teacher William Cullen (1710-1790), but eventually turned against his mentor to develop his idiosyncratic medical ideas as part of an overall attempt to simplify and reduce some of the multiple contradictions in eighteenth century medical theory.[10] Brown argued that the complex nosologies and dubious practice of eighteenth century medicine could be cut away by reducing all diseases to questions of either over-stimulation or under-stimulation in the body's tonic system. Diseases were thus sthenic or asthenic, depending on which side of the equilibrial line a patient had come to lie. Over- or under-excitement: this was the central cause of disease, to be treated with stimulants or depressants as the case required. In seeking to reduce and simplify the disease concepts of the eighteenth century, Brown hoped to solve finally a complex riddle that a number of eighteenth century medical writers had noted.

Mitchill and Beddoes were both attracted to the Brunonian system. Even though both men felt it to be exaggerated in some aspects, there remained a common interest, as we can see in the discussions in the <u>Medical Repository</u>, a magazine founded in 1797 and edited by Mitchill. The exchanges focus on the agency of diseases, and in turn on what other agents might be used to stimulate, or depress, a patient under the canons of the Brunonian method. As we know, Beddoes came to place his faith in gases to perform this task. But part of his faith must have come from the creative damage that Humphry Davy effected on a particularly peculiar thesis of Mitchill's.

Seeking, like many eighteenth century doctors, for a single underlying cause to disease, a search much encouraged by John Brown and taken to its limit

by Mitchill's countryman Benjamin Rush, Mitchill
proposed, in a pamphlet entitled <u>Remarks on the
Gaseous Oxyd of Azote or of Nitrogen</u> of 1795, that
all infectious diseases were caused by the action on
the organs of this 'gaseous oxyd of azote'. He
argues that life was enhanced and vivified by oxygen,
but destroyed and dissolved by its opposite, which
was nitrous oxide, or what Mitchill called 'Septon'.
Mitchill's crude divisions of vivifying and depress-
ing powers, to which all human life was exposed,
reflects the Brunonian division of stimulation and
depression as the cause of disease. Nitrous oxide
for Mitchill (or 'oxide of septon' as he called it)
caused widespread fever because it was present in the
miasma of decaying vegetation and thus poisoned
the air of large tracts of country. Contagion and
fever were explained by the presence of this 'great
Disorganiser', Septon. In typical eighteenth
century manner, aping the style of Erasmus Darwin,
Mitchill set out his thesis in the form of a poem,
which he sent to Beddoes in Oxford on September 15th
1797. It was reprinted in <u>The Medical Repository</u>
that same year.[11] We hear first of all that:

> Man's constitution thus full well ye knew
> From Oxygen its life and vigour drew;
> Whence tinctured all its grosser parts
>   refine;

But a moment later arrives:

> Grim Septon, arm'd with power to intervene
> And disconnect the animal machine:

It may be of some interest to note that Mitchill believed that alkalis should be utilised to prevent the defeat of life at the hands of the septic principle.

Now, as we know from F.F. Cartwright and others,[12] it was this bizarre thesis that the young Davy, who had probably seen a copy of Mitchill's 1795 article as an appendix to Beddoes' <u>Considerations on Factitious Airs</u> at Giddy's home at Tredrea, set out to disprove. This cannot be isolated as a 'chemical' achievement. Davy's exposing animal wounds to crude nitrous oxide, and his eventually breathing this apparently lethal gas in large amounts, was also a medical advance. The young Davy not only reversed the hypothesis of the Professor of Chemistry, Natural History and Agriculture in the College of New York: he even gave Beddoes, as it were, a Brunonian gift - a gas that contributed to the new medical programme, but now as a stimulant and vivifier, and not as a lethal, contagious agent of destruction. That both Davy and Beddoes came to be disenchanted with the claims of nitrous oxide does not detract from the fact that an untrained apothecary's apprentice from Penzance had made a bold contribution to a radical medical theory, in an institutional setting that was a unique attempt to put that theory into practice. I leave aside the problems of Davy's recommendations for using the gas as an anaesthetic, problems related to a failure by both Beddoes and Davy to maintain sufficient oxygen proportions when experimenting with the gas (qv. E.B. Smith, pp. 231-237).

As we know, Humphry Davy's interests from then on became increasingly concentrated on issues of chemistry and galvanism, and of course on light and heat, some of his earlier investigations in this area being of considerable embarrassment to him. His theory of respiration still remains an astonishing melange of Hartley, Cavendish and Lavoisier, with its mysterious 'phos-oxygen' lighting up the brain. Moreover, once in London, at least in Morris Berman's view, Davy became both the lion of the Royal Institution and the servant of the improving agricultural interest that dominated the management of the R.I. in the early years of its history.[13]

What I have tried to suggest is that the _young_ Davy is also the _medical_ Davy, and to suggest that an unconsummated relationship to medicine forms part of that unfocussed element in Davy's general career that many writers have noted. For in Clifton especially he was clearly involved in medical activity, along with Beddoes' other assistants; William Clayfield, the physician Kinglake, and the surgeon from Berne, John King. It is worth saying more about King, since involvement with the idiosyncratic world of Thomas Beddoes seems to have exacted quite a considerable price, and not on Beddoes alone. The degeneration of the Pneumatic Institution into the more orthodox ways of preventive medicine did not kill off Beddoes' hopes for medical reform entirely; but in the case of John King, there is a real sense of someone being beached as the tide went out on applied Brunonian medicine, even though King did also favour 'traditional' cures, such as digitalis, often to the chagrin of his more radical mentor Beddoes.

King left Switzerland in 1791, having attempted to enter a medical career against the wishes of his patrician family. He reached London in 1791/2, and became a pupil of John Abernethy (1764-1831) at St. Bartholomew's. Abernethy also had some interesting speculations on the prospects of a chemical revolution coming to influence the practice of medicine. We do not know whether John King ever fully qualified in medicine, and his arrival at Clifton has the same half-achieved relationship to physic that we have noted in Davy's case. King married (like Beddoes) into the Edgeworth family, and practiced surgery in Clifton until his death in August 1846. He was well-known in the Bristol art world for his drawings and engravings; he also made little attempt to hide his aetheism. What is striking about King's life is its relative poverty, its loyalty to Beddoes to the end, and its general sense of marginality. Davy corresponded with King from London, in letters redolent of a sentimental idea of Clifton, of Hotwells, and its 'old ideas': for King the truth was harder.

Beddoes at least knew this; in a letter of 23rd August 1805 to Davies Gilbert, he writes:[14]

> I have heard with concern that King has little or nothing to do and that this has been the case for pretty much some time - I think his situation in the Hotwells is pretty much unfavourable, in as much as, my own single case excepted, everything depends upon cabal and correspondence. Now I suppose King has nobody to cabal for him and scarce a correspondent in the world to send him patients... I fear he is not likely to see better times upon the whole - and if he has paid his way it is the utmost - and behold a family that threatens to increase fast ...

King was well known for his generosity, his lack of powerful friends and contacts with large, rich families, and his reluctance to chase up those who failed to pay him for his services. His case must also suggest that Davy, by coming to London, was rescued from a rapidly declining medical world in Clifton, with all the legacy of ambivalence that this implies.

Davy left Bristol and Penzance, but before looking on to the curious Cambridge episode of 1804/5, we need to look back at his home town to see what

developments there had been. The historian of Penzance, P.A.S.Pool, shows us that culturally Penzance developed considerably from 1800 onwards.[15] The rights to mint coinage, the profitability of the pier and market, as well as its fishing activities, all indicate economic stability. Of the various institutional indicators that sprang up - the Assembly Rooms of 1791, the Royal Geological Society of 1814, and the Library of 1818, to name but three - one is of especial interest. This was the Penzance Public Dispensary and Humane Society, founded in 1809. The setting up of dispensaries in early nineteenth century England as part of a charitable reaction to fears of popular impoverishment is a subject of historical interest.[16] What is important about the Penzance Dispensary, is that its founding physician was John Bingham Borlase, to whom Davy had been apprenticed; that his successor in 1813 was the physician and mineralogist John Ayrton Paris; and that at one time, Humphry's brother John was at the point of taking up a position there. In an intriguing blend of historical coincidence, John Davy's interest fell away because he was delayed in returning to England by Napoleon's vacillation as when to join battle with Wellington at Waterloo.[17]
John Davy eventually settled to a career of colonial medicine, having also discussed the possibility (orchestrated by his brother) of going to the Nottingham Infirmary.[18]

In setting up the Penzance Dispensary, the upper class and clergy (both Dissenting and Anglican) and medical men of West Cornwall may well have been following advice propogated by Thomas Beddoes, when he had argued in 1791 <u>against</u> a Cornish <u>Infirmary</u> on the grounds that it failed to assist the immobilised poor, and was more likely to promote the spread of contagious diseases, given the number of patients under a single roof. Instead, Beddoes favoured dispensaries and, where necessary, the bringing 'of Physicians to Patients.'[19] This, however, did not stop the setting up of the hospital in Truro in the 1790s which had 47 in-patients by 1800. Like all infirmaries, diseases like VD were regarded as 'improper' and not dealt with, this disease being one that Beddoes had hoped to cure by using nitrous acid. In Penzance, on the other hand, the Dispensary appears to have been very active, and one of its historians, Dr. E.C. Edwards, reckoned that J.B. Borlase had dealt with about 1,733 patients in his four years in the Dispensary. The dominant diseases appear to have been rheumatism, fever, and amenorrehia; with surgery required for fractures, particularly numerous in a mining community.[20]

When J.A. Paris became the Dispensary physician in 1813, he organized for the physician's room to be used by the Geological Society, and made considerable attempts to promote mineralogy as well as medicine in Penzance, hoping at one time to become a Professor of Mineralogy to the Royal Geological Society of Cornwall. Paris was frustrated in his aims, despite the apparent lucrativeness of his Cornish practice, and it may be that an underlying bitterness from his Penzance years seeps through in his biography of Davy.[21] There can be little doubt that had Davy taken Tonkin's advice, he would have dominated this local world of medicine and science, of which the Penzance Dispensary formed a central part. After all, the Dispensary originally began in Market Jew Street, and Humphry's mother received £14 per annum rent from the institution in its early years. Not the least of the Dispensary's merits is that its records allow us to see the activities of the otherwise unreachable John Bingham Borlase, whose death in 1813 is recorded in the minute books as 'an event that will long be deplored.'[22]

Despite the death of Borlase, Penzance generated a modest but active general culture. Two later physicians at the Dispensary, for example, were John Forbes from 1817-1822, and Henry Boase from 1822-1826. Forbes (1787-1861) became distinguished in later life, and in his years at Penzance worked on the medical topography of Penwith, and on the climate of Penzance, following in this last work some of the perspectives developed by J.A. Paris in the latter's <u>Guide to Mount's Bay and Land's End.</u> Forbes went on to found the infirmary in Chichester in Sussex in 1827, and became a well-known editor of the 'British and Foreign Medical Review' and an investigator of mesmeric practices in medicine. It was while he was in Penzance that he translated the great work of the French physician Laënnec, 'Mediate Auscultation', with its description of the newly invented stethoscope. Henry Boase was both a physician in Penzance, an active evangelical follower of the Lancastrian educational system, and a promoter of the town's first savings bank.

Both these men, and others such as the surgeon Henry Penneck (parodied by J.A. Paris in his book <u>Philosophy in Sport made Science in Earnest</u> of 1827 as Dr. DOSEALL), participated in a local world of orthodox medicine, coupled with a commitment to increasing scientific research, especially on local geology and mineralogy. Penzance would be particularly interesting to doctors such as Forbes, interested in the relations between climate, consumption and so on. Mention might also be made of John Edwards of Hayle Copper House, whose chemical apparatus Davy had seen as a young man, and who went on, from being an energetic entrepreneur in Hayle, to a chemical lectureship at St.Bartholomew's Hospital.

The records of the Penzance Dispensary suggest conventional methods of leeching, coupled with a commitment to introducing smallpox vaccination. In so far as relations between chemistry and medicine were concerned, J.A. Paris suggested that pharmaceut-icals would benefit most. For Davy the relationship between chemistry and medicine was more spectacular.

By becoming involved in the pneumatics movement, the boy who had mixed medicines for a surgeon-apothecary had advanced to the far limits of both sciences, and seemed finally settled for a chemical career once Count Rumford had brought him to London. If he was to find his way back into medical life, his unorthodox early career might prove an obstacle. In addition, Davy seems to have been an unusual and rather good geologist, and must have picked up considerable mineralogical experience in Penzance and Bristol. Would either skill be developed further in the world of metropolitan science?

On the question of his skills in mineralogy, and then on agricultural chemistry, others must speak. As both Bence-Jones and Berman have shown, Davy's early career at the R.I. was linked quite clearly to these sciences. With regard to medicine, the situation remains mysterious. Berman's history shows clearly that the period when the R.I. developed its links between chemistry and medicine coincides with the period after the Apothecaries Act of 1815, and occurred under the tutelage of William Thomas Brande. Henry Bence-Jones, himself a pupil at St.George's Hospital, attended Brande's morning lectures on chemistry, designed for medical students.[23] The link between the R.I. and medicine was _not_ made under Davy's aegis. We do know however that Davy encouraged Sir Francis Baring to introduce degrees in medicine in the London Institution. In a letter of October 3rd of 1805, Davy says that an institution in London that provided a medical training would make it easier for men who were at present

> ... obliged either to pass six or seven years at Oxford or Cambridge where there is no good opportunity of passing medical studies, or of making the long journey so as to attend the classes for three winters at Edinburgh.[24]

Davy was particularly aware of this last point, since he had organized the funding of his brother's medical education at Edinburgh. He also told Baring that it would benefit the popularity both of the Medical schools in London and of the institutions providing medical and chemical lectures.

Now all this occurred in 1805, a year when we know that Davy felt pessimistic about the advancement of chemistry through the medium of lectures at the R.I.[25] It is possible therefore that Davy was either seriously thinking of committing himself to a medical career, or, less ambitiously, was conceding that although the Royal Institution might not carry the lectures, at least some metropolitan scientific organization should. It is also worth reminding ourselves that Davy originally enrolled at Cambridge before he was appointed, in February 1805, Director of the Laboratory at the R.I., with a guaranteed income of £400. His flirtation with a return to medicine may have cooled as a result of this appointment. Whatever the reasons, Davy's career pattern in 1804-5 can now be seen as remarkably fluid.

The extent of his activities in Cambridge are impossible to gauge; he enrolled as a Gentleman Commoner at Jesus, which gave him certain dining rights, and one of his three tutors was the man who became Cambridge's first Professor of Mineralogy in 1808, Edward Daniel Clarke. Clarke's papers make no mention of Davy's presence in Cambridge. What they do make clear is that Clarke enjoyed a close friendship with his biographer-to-be William Otter and with the Rev. T.R. Malthus, these three forming a tight circle from which Davy may have been excluded. The Master of Jesus at this time, the Cornishman William Pearce, increased the Cornish intake to the College, as its records show. It seems perfectly reasonable to assume that Davy would have been unimpressed with the state of medical education at Cambridge in 1804 and 1805. This had also been the view of another professor at the R.I., Thomas Young (1773-1829), who did however come to practise as a physician in London from 1799. Perhaps Davy saw Young's experience as a model, but one that he could not imitate. He may, as a result of his glance at Busick Harwood's Cambridge, also have come to share Young's pessimism on the state of medicine.

Humphry Davy's career then, at least up to 1807, must be seen in a more contingent and open-ended setting. My argument is that the crucial dimension that had remained unsettled was his relationship to medicine, since it was that world which seemed to guarantee an income. Humphry was certainly pleased that his brother John was a medical man - we may recall his letter of October 1811 when he joked to John that he (John) 'would be a rich physician and I a poor gunpowder merchant', referring here to his collaboration with J.G. Children (1777-1852).[26] John Davy's career indicates an amalgamation of chemical training, much of it learnt at the R.I. under Humphry's guidance, with a medical career. John lectured on chemistry at the Medical School in Windmill Street, taking over from W.T. Brande. In later life, he even came to establish a dispensary, but one far from Penzance: it was in fact in Valetta, when he was President of the Medical Council of the University of Malta in the mid-1830s.[27]

Davy's unresolved relationship to medicine can be partly explained, I suggest, by his involvement with the idiosyncratic medical programme of Beddoes, one that ensured the absence of a full-time education at a recognised medical teaching establishment in Britain. Although not himself an anti-establishment figure, indeed the reverse, Davy was indebted to the medical uses of chemistry that brought him to Beddoes' attention, but was faced with a commitment of five years or more if he was to re-enter the field in later life. The years that brought this issue to a head are also ones that Morris Berman has seen as difficult for the Royal

Institution as well, and especially Davy's place in it. In that sense, Davy's career reflects a double ambivalence, both to medicine and to the metropolitan institution that brought him to fame. That these tensions were resolved does not lessen their historical interest, especially if one adds the importance of his marriage to a wealthy widow and the subsequent early retirement from the mainstream of London life.[28]

This finally makes Davy's centrality as a Romantic philosopher even more important. In the classical environment of Rome, he envisioned a philosophical idea of great power and individuality, with elements of natural, historical and scientific imagination completing the synthesis. One might, without exaggeration, call it a Boethian achievement, with its promise of an old idea of philosophy: consolation. For that is also the word that Beddoes had used in his adieu to his one time protégé. Davy wrote,[29]

> On his death, [Beddoes] wrote me a most affecting letter regretting his scientific aberrations. I remember one expression: 'like one who has scattered abroad the avena fatua of knowledge, from which neither branch, nor bloom nor fruit has resulted, I require the consolation of a friend.'

NOTES

For their help and criticism in the preparation of this article, I wish to thank Bill Bynum, Roy Porter and Mary-Kay Wilmers. I owe a particular debt to Christopher Lawrence.

1. See *British Journal for the History of Science*, 9 (July 1976), which contains various commemorative essays on Lyell, and seeks revisions of his own estimate of the history of geology, especially the article by Roy Porter, 'Charles Lyell and the Principles of the History of Geology'. See also W.F. Bynum, 'Charles Lyell and the *Antiquity of Man*', *Victorian Studies* (forthcoming).
2. *Memoirs*, vol.1, p.277.
3. R.I. Davy Ms, Book 13c, 'Memoirs on Anthroponomia or the Laws of Human Nature'.
4. *Memoirs*, vol.2, p.368.
5. Ibid., vol.1, pp.425-426.
6. H. Mayhew, *The Wonders of Science*, London, 1860, p.419.
7. See the forthcoming volume edited by I. Inkster and J.B. Morrell, *Metropolis and Province: studies in nineteenth century scientific culture*, London, 1980.

8. The only exception to this statement is Davy's paper on the geology of Cornwall, in the Transactions of the Royal Geological Society of Cornwall, 1 (1818), 38-50.
9. See J. Rowe, Cornwall in the Age of the Industrial Revolution, London, p.68.
10. On Cullen see J. Thomson, An Account of the life, lectures and writings of William Cullen, Edinburgh, 1832. On Brown, see Thomas Beddoes' translation of The Elements of Medicine, London, 1795. On Beddoes, see J.E. Stock, Memoirs of the Life of Thomas Beddoes, M.D., London, 1811.
11. See the biography of Mitchill by C.R. Hall, A scientist in the early republic, New York, 1934; also Sidney M. Edelstein, 'The chemical revolution in America from the pages of the 'Medical Repository', Chymia, 5 (1959), 155-179.
12. F.F. Cartwright, The English Pioneers of Anaesthesia, Bristol, 1952. See also A.C. Todd, Beyond the Blaze, Truro, 1967.
13. M. Berman, Social Change and Scientific Organization: The Royal Institution 1799-1844, London and Ithaca, 1978, pp.32-74.
14. Davies Gilbert Archive, Cornwall County Record Office, MS/DG 43. For John King, see the manuscript collection in the Bristol Record Office, ref. no. 32688/31.
15. See his History of the Town and Borough of Penzance, 1974.

16. The forthcoming work of Dr. I.S.L. Louden on the dispensaries of London from 1750 should be particularly illuminating in this regard.
17. Letter dated 1 June 1815, from H. Davy to Miss E. Davy, in Penzance; R.I. Davy Ms, Box 26 B/7.
18. Letter from Humphry Davy to John Davy, dated Nottingham, 6 August 1820; R.I. Davy Ms, Box 26 B/8.
19. Stock, op.cit. (10), Appendix 3.
20. Penzance Dispensary Minute Book, 1803-1828, Cornwall County Record Office, Truro, DDX/439, accession number, 1848. E.C. Edwards, *A History of the West Cornwall Hospital*, Penzance, 1974, passim. Borlase briefly attended the Infirmary at Bristol, but had to resign; see G. Munro Smith, *A History of the Bristol Royal Infirmary*, Bristol, 1917, pp.99-100.
21. This can be detected reading the entry in the *D.N.B.*, written by Norman Moore.
22. Penzance Dispensary Minute Book, 1803-1828, loc.cit. (20).
23. Quoted from Berman, op.cit. (13), p.135.
24. R.I. Davy Ms, Box 22C, p.126.
25. Ibid., Box 22C, p.41.
26. Ibid., Box 26B, p.18.

27. John Davy, 'Some Notices of My Life', MS kept in the Archives Department at the University of Keele, Staffs. I am grateful to the Archivist at Keele for permission to quote from this manuscript.
28. A point made well in Cartwright, op.cit. (12), pp.249-250.
29. Quoted from Anne Treneer, The Mercurial Chemist, London, 1963, p.113, from a letter to Davy of 1808.

Humphry Davy, 'The Sons of Genius', and the Idea of Glory

Trevor H. Levere

Davy, in his youth and prime, numbered among his regular correspondents the great Swedish chemist Berzelius, and Samuel Taylor Coleridge, poet, philosopher, and enthusiast for Romantic science. Berzelius, who after Davy's death called him the greatest chemist of his time, had been critical of him for his lack of discipline and system. Thorough, precise, and clear, Berzelius demanded these same virtues in others. Davy's ready and casual use of hypotheses and his broad imaginative purview were antipathetic to the Swede, who found the style of Davy's <u>Elements of Chemical Philosophy</u> intensely frustrating. 'Great minds often attach too little importance to details ... Your philosophy is too far above my criticism,' he complained to Davy. The result, in Berzelius's view, was that Davy 'left only brilliant fragments'.[1]

Davy left more than brilliant fragments, but even those were informed by unifying ideas of the order and simplicity of nature and of the connection, perhaps unity, of chemical and electrical powers.

Coleridge, lacking all scientific training but eager to explore the dynamic unity of nature and the role of ideas in science, apostrophized Davy as 'the Father and Founder of philosophic Alchemy, the Man who <u>born</u> a Poet first converted Poetry into Science and <u>realized</u> what few men possessed Genius enough to <u>fancy</u>'. Davy's chemistry, thus perceived, was simply poetry realized in nature, and Davy, after Wordsworth, was for Coleridge the greatest man of the age.[2]

That two such different men as Coleridge and Berzelius recognized Davy's greatness says something about the range of his achievement and the sympathies it excited. Davy's aspirations were certainly boundless. After a local education, valuable principally for leaving his mind untrammelled, he formulated a plan of study as revealing as it was impossible of realisation. He would master theology, geography, botany, pharmacology, nosology, anatomy, surgery, chemistry, logic, half a dozen dead and living languages, physics, mechanics, rhetoric and oratory, history, chronology, and mathematics.[3]

When he moved to Bristol to work under Beddoes's direction, he expanded this program to give more emphasis to poetry and to metaphysics, and made a '<u>Resolution</u> ... To work two hours with pen before breakfast on the 'Lover of Nature; and 'The Feelings of Eldon', from six till eight; from nine till two, in experiments; from four to six, reading; seven till ten, metaphysical reading (i,e, system of the universe)'.[4] Davy's new-found devotion to the writing of epic poetry was encouraged by Robert Southey. Davy responded vigorously, sending him plans and drafts of poems for criticism, and submitting poems for publication in Southey's <u>Annual Anthology</u>.[5] The first volume of this would-be annual contained Davy's 'Sons of Genius', boldly expressing his personal and scientific aspirations:

> While Superstition rules the vulgar soul,
>   Forbids the energies of man to ride,
> Raised far above her low, her mean controul,
>   Aspiring Genius seeks her native skies.
> ......
>
> To scan the laws of Nature, to explore
>   The tranquil reign of mild Philosophy;
> Or on Newtonian wings sublime to soar
>   Through the bright regions of the
>   starry sky.
> ......
>
> From these pursuits the Sons of Genius scan
>   The end of their creation; hence they know
> The fair, sublime, immortal hopes of man,
>   From whence alone undying pleasures glow.
> ......
>
> Like the tumultuous billows of the sea
>   Succeed the generations of mankind;
> Some in oblivious silence pass away,
>   And leave no vestige of their lives
>   behind.
> ......
>
> Like you proud rocks amidst the sea of time,
>   Superior, scorning all the billows' rage,
> The living Sons of Genius stand sublime,
>   Th' immortal children of another age.[6]

This was practically Davy's manifesto and his career plan. He knew that he was a genius, destined for glory and immortality through imperishable discoveries, and he dreamed of becoming the Newton of chemistry - Dalton subsequently emerged as the Kepler in this scenario. Genius was a preoccupation of Romantic poets and philosophers - but it was scarcely their private preserve.

The aspirations of genius fired Davy's ambitions for himself, his science, and his country. True glory was to be achieved through science. Politics and warfare might lead to temporary eminence, but advances in science led to the highest honours and distinctions, for these alone endured. Genius was, moreover, God-given, unlike merely temporal dignity. 'Persons of very exalted talents and virtues', Davy remarked, 'may be said to derive their patent of nobility directly from God; and their titles are not registered in perishable court calendars, but written in the great histories of Nature or of Man'. In his last work, <u>Consolations in Travel, or, The Last Days of a Philosopher,</u> Davy put into the mouth of that work's hero, the all but autobiographical Unknown, a description of man enobled and civilized through science, taming the earth and subduing it to his needs and comforts, 'perpetuating thought in imperishable words, rendering immortal the exertions of genius and presenting them as common property to all awakening minds, - becoming as it were the true image of divine intelligence receiving and bestowing the breath of life in the influence of civilisation'.[7] In 'The Sons of Genius', written in or around 1795, the scientist of genius was portrayed as one above mere terrestrial cares; thirty-five years later, Davy had come to see the material benefits deriving from the applications of science as important concerns of even the purest natural philosopher.

But whether immortality sprung from the abstracted contemplation of nature, or from the triumphs of applied science, glory accrued to scientists of genius. The point may be illustrated by the contrast that Davy postulated between projectors and other alchemical charlatans on the one hand, and '<u>true alchemical philosophers</u>' on the other. The latter, Davy argued, 'had often sublime and elevated views. The idea of glory was continually present to them. To ameliorate the condition of humanity, and to support the interests of religion, were constantly held out as their objects.... [T]heir errors were the errors natural to an infant science; but their industry was unceasing, their <u>hopes glorious</u>, and their discoveries eminently useful'. The emergence in Davy of a marriage of the concepts of utility and glory enabled him to lecture on agricultural chemistry and to adopt the entrepreneurial ideology demonstrated by Morris Berman as characterizing the first decades of the Royal Institution, while at the same time sharing Romantic concerns with genius, creativity, and the harmony of nature.[8]

It was this facet of Davy's receptive mind that made him so eager and responsive first to Southey, and afterwards to Coleridge and Wordsworth. Their admiration of him as a scientific prodigy could not but season his responsiveness. Southey left it to Davy to revise and publish his long poem 'Thalaba, the Destroyer'. Wordsworth and Coleridge sought his aid in seeing their <u>Lyrical Ballads</u> through the press, and Wordsworth in the preface to that work addressed Davy about the respective claims and language of science and poetry.[9] Walter Scott was to write after Davy's death that he 'would have established himself in the first ranks of England's living poets, if the Genius of our country had not decreed that he should rather be the first in the first rank of its philosophers and scientific benefactors'. Only Southey's epitaph for Davy was perhaps ambivalent, stating that 'he had all the elements of a poet; he only wanted the art'.[10]

Art or skill aside, Davy was convinced that great powers were necessarily accompanied by intense feelings; he planned, as we have seen, to write a poem entitled 'The Lover of Nature'; he adopted the stance, albeit in semi-fiction, that wildness was part of the true poetical temperament; and he agreed with his fiancée that mountain scenery exalted the imagination. His 'Sons of Genius' were <u>above</u> all

material cares precisely because of their love of
nature, and they dutifully delighted not only in
the pastoral, but also in nature's grand scenes, the
great, the sublime, and the terrible. In 'The
Sybil's Temple', inspired by a visit to Tivoli on
his first continental tour, Davy wrote of a sublime
sympathy with natural forms and sounds, in which the
mind 'forgets/Its present being'.[11]

All the ingredients are present for the
construction a sociologist's extinct dream, the ideal
type of the Romantic poet. But one may come to
suspect that much of Davy's Romantic inspiration lay
in his enthusiastic desire to emulate his friends
the Lake Poets, and that his delight in nature was
more that of the scientist and fly-fisherman than
that of the poet. 'Oh, most magnificent and noble
Nature!' he exclaimed in a notebook,

> Have I not worshipped thee with such a love
> As never mortal man before displayed?
> Adored thee in thy majesty of visible
>   creation,
> And searched into thy hidden and mysterious
>   ways
> As Poet, as Philosopher, as Sage?[12]

The natural philosopher's love of nature for its law-
abiding harmonies was truly Davy's own. Poetic
imagination was there too, but needing more deliberate cultivation. He succeeded, not long after 1795,
in experiencing a poetic experience at once Romantic
and Spinozistic. 'To-day, for the first time in my

life', he recorded, 'I have had a distinct sympathy with nature. I was lying on the top of a rock to leeward; the wind was high, and everything in motion...; everything was alive, and myself part of the series of visible impressions' - visible impressions smack more of Hartley and Locke than of Wordsworth, and a later addition to this notebook entry completes the transition from Romantic poet to scientist. 'Deeply and intimately connected', Davy concluded, 'are all our ideas of motion and life, and this, probably, from very early association. How different is the idea of life in a physiologist and a poet!'[13]

The difference became for Davy not merely one of kind, but also one of value. By the time that he was lecturing on geology at the Royal Institution, he has clearly subordinated poetic to scientific pleasures. 'The image of a mountain country, which is the very theatre of the science', he told his audience, 'is, in almost all cases, highly impressive and delightful; but a new and nobler species of enjoyment arises in the mind when the arrangement in it, it uses and its subserviency to life, are considered'. Increasingly, he came to see poetry as but a vehicle for transitory pleasure, while science was enduring, beautiful, useful, and true. In 1812 Davy, lecturing on electrochemistry, asserted that all knowledge was acquired by the senses, and that 'Nature has no archetype in the human imagination'.[14]

Here was a rejection of a philosophical position shared by many Romantics, cogently developed in England by Coleridge, who was in this going well beyond Schelling's Naturphilosophie. Schelling had presented natural phenomena as the limited products of developing mind.[15] For Coleridge, there was a sense in which nature could be regarded as constituted by ideas of mind; laws of nature and ideas of reason thus exhibited a congruence based on their underlying unity. Given the intimate connection between Coleridge's conception of reason and imagination, this was as much as to say that nature did have its archetype in the human imagination. Davy, denying this, was effectively disjoining himself from whole traditions of idealistic philosophy. He was as clear as could be about the need for that disjunction, while hazy about recent developments in Germany, where, he complained, 'the metaphysical dogmas of Kant which as far as I can learn are pseudo platonism are preferred before the doctrines of Locke and Hartley, excellence and knowledge being rather sought for in the infant than in the adult state of mind'.[16]

His revulsion against philosophies outside British empiricism was accompanied by the recognition that he was to be a scientist, a natural and especially a chemical philosopher, and not a poet. Underneath a prospectus that he drew up for a volume of poems, he wrote definitively:

> These were the visions of my youth
> Which fled before the voice of truth.[17]

His removal from Bristol to the Royal Institution took him from the society of poets, radicals, and democrats, to the society of established landowners imbued with an entrepreneurial ideology of science new in England although already held by the improving landlords of Scotland and, albeit more theoretically, by the philosophers and virtuosi of the French and the prior English Enlightenment. Only now, with an expanding population and scarcity of grain for bread and of oak bark for tanning leather for shoes, - with an economy still in the throes of industrial revolution, and with the need to arm and organize society in the face of fears of French invasion, - only now did the ideology of science gain a new dynamic. Berman has shown how the Royal Institution was in the vanguard of this process. Shared aims and, even more significantly, a substantial overlap between the membership of the Board of Agriculture and the early governance of the Royal Institution, soon led the latter body into the more remunerative aspects of agricultural development.[18]

The Royal Institution in its first decade was, in short, precisely the foundation in which science emerged as a directing force in society; and it did so with the co-operation of great landowners and leading Fellows of the Royal Society, including its president, but in a far more equivocal relation to other commercial interests. Davy's appointment to the Royal Institution gave immediate and tremendous scope to his ambitions and abilities, neither of which he had ever sought to disguise.

Davy responded eagerly and shrewdly to the genteel audience and new social sphere to which his responsibilities now introduced him. Coleridge, himself a more fundamental critic of society, was disillusioned, even appalled, at what he saw as Davy's apostasy from youthful radical ideals. He feared that Davy's promise might be strangled by the serpent of ambition, and complained that Davy moulded himself more and more upon the age, so that the age might mould itself upon him.[19] But in a way that Coleridge totally failed to comprehend, Davy's ambition fired his enthusiasm for scientific research. Shortly after his promotion to Lecturer in Chemistry at the Royal Institution, Davy wrote to his old friend John King, working with Beddoes in Bristol: 'The voice of fame is murmuring in my ear - My mind has been excited by the unexpected plaudits of the multitude - I dream of greatness and utility - I dream of science restoring to Nature what Luxury, what civilization have stolen from her - pure hearts, the forme of angels, bosoms beautiful; and panting with joy and hope.... So much for egotism - for weak, glorious, pitiful, sublime, conceited egotism.'[20] Coleridge could only hope that Davy's intellectual powers would protect his moral character. 'There does not exist,' he remarked hopefully, 'an instance of a _deep_ metaphysician who was not led by his speculations to an austere system of morals'. He continued to fear for Davy's morals.[21]

Davy, for his part, saw his chance, and seized it. He had begun admiring Newton and the pure intellectual light of scientific discovery, had gone on to work under Beddoes in an attempt to develop chemical and medical knowledge in the service of mankind, and had then been translated to London by Rumford, part-time philanthropist, entrepreneur, and adventurer extraordinary. Now, at the Royal Institution, he was called upon to give chemical lectures to the higher classes, to advise the Board of Agriculture on technical scientific matters, and to develop a research program in chemistry. This experience and these aims were not mutually contradictory. One needed only to appeal to Francis Bacon's notion of science yielding both fruit and light, material and intellectual benefits, in order to see how Davy's experience could serve his ambition. It was not so much, if at all, that Davy was malleable and so a serviceable tool for the landowners; instead, their ideology and his own proved compatible. The time he spent on applied research, and the cost of such equipment as platinum crucibles or a voltaic pile of two thousand plates, suggests that the Managers were as convinced of the importance of experiments of light as Davy was of the need for experiments of fruit.[22]

Davy's greatest initial contributions were in chemical science in its intellectual rather than utilitarian aspects. He attacked the theory of caloric, developed a theory of the relation of chemical to electrical action that was at least susceptible of a dynamic interpretation, and assailed Lavoisier's table of the chemical elements. Seeking, as Coleridge had urged, for an understanding of power and arrangement in chemistry, he used the Voltaic pile, discovered in 1800, as a source of polar power to investigate bodies.[23] The discoveries he made and his lectures about them delighted Coleridge, who sought and found in Davy's researches confirmation of philosophical views, and visible symbols of poetical truths. Chemistry in England and France was, in the early 1800s, based on an essentially mechanical philosophy, to which Dalton's atomic theory gave succinct expression. Such a system makes it hard to account for chemical qualities, or reactions, or relations between reactants and products. A contemporary alternative to atomic chemistry was a dynamical chemistry, based upon powers and their mutual modifications and relations, in conformity with the universal law of polarity. Coleridge, elaborating this alternative, saw the chemical elements of the laboratory as symbols of polar powers, whose dynamic reconciliation constituted chemical combination. The Nature Philosophers of Germany, metaphysical heretics in most English eyes, recognized the over-riding importance of polarity in chemistry, philosophy, and all of physical and mental nature.[24]

Schelling and his followers were scarcely empiricist philistines. Even those among them most skilled in experiment were given to confusing theory with fact. Johan Wilhelm Ritter, the author of extensive galvanical researches, was typical in this respect. German Romantics came to regard him as the supreme authority in science. Clemens Brentano, for example, urged his sister: 'Write to Ritter as you would write to the universe. He is about to spell out the creation'.[25] Davy, however, while given to great theorizing, was condescending about Ritter's errors as a theorist, extracting empirical nuggets from accounts of Ritter's work, and discounting everything else. Coleridge shared Davy's unease at German failures adequately to distinguish the speculative from the empirical, and came for a while to see Davy as the only hope for dynamic and Romantic chemistry.

Davy seemed, after all, to adhere to a dynamical theory of matter - at any rate, he discussed chemical reactions in terms of forces, and was interested in Boscovich's and Priestley's theories that matter was essentially force. He also knew and, at least for a while, admired Bishop Berkeley's writings: and Berkeley, as Coleridge saw it, 'needed only an entire instead of a partial emancipation from the fetters of the mechanic philosophy in order to have enunciated all that is true and important in modern Chemistry'. Davy was, in short, well prepared intellectually, and this, with his undoubted genius in the laboratory, made him the ideal man in England to accomplish the much needed reform of chemistry.

This, at least, was how Coleridge first saw it. Not only was Davy using polar power - current electricity - to probe the relations of bodies, but, for reasons metaphysical and theological, he believed in the order, unity, and simplicity of the natural world. Lavoisier's table of elements, published in 1789, was neither rationally ordered, nor simple. It was, moreover, French, and an enemy invention.[26]

Davy, imbued with eighteenth-century English philosophy, natural theology, and patriotic fervour, tinged ever so lightly with second-hand German metaphysics, and armed with electrical power and the conviction of his own genius, probed the weakest parts of Lavoisier's table. In his early lectures, following his experiments on the amalgamation of ammonia, he argued that nitrogen was not a simple body, but could be converted to oxygen and another, hitherto unknown substance, related to the principle common to all the metals. This fitted well with German philosophical and dynamic chemistry, and not at all with corpuscular chemistry. It was also, unhappily, based on faulty analyses.[27]

Not all Davy's attacks on Lavoisier's table were delusive. His successes in 1806 and 1807 were dramatic, and his experimental demonstrations beauti-ful in their logic and style. The chemical action of electricity was partially elucidated, and the caustic alkalis shown to be compound - all in a manner further supportive of dynamism, however casual and shifting Davy's commitment to dynamism must have been.

Coleridge was positively exalted by the discovery of the alkali metals – Davy's 'March of Glory' had led him to 'discoveries more intellectual, more enobling and impowering human Nature, than Newton's!' Berzelius called the paper 'one of the best ... which has ever enriched the theory of chemistry'. Even Brougham paid tribute through the critical <u>Edinburgh Review</u>.[28]

Davy was certainly fulfilling his ambition 'on Newtonian wings sublime to soar'. It is ironic that even his most striking discoveries brought tribulation. Alas, in discovering sodium and potassium, far from exposing greater simplicity in nature, he added to the number of chemical elements. His fame as a chemical philosopher rested largely upon the contradiction of his beliefs, beliefs made explicit in his lectures. 'It seems very probable', he wrote, 'from the past ⟦process⟧ of discovery- ... That the number of elements will be diminished: and that arrangements of a very simple nature will explain these phenomena which are now referred to complicated and diversified agents'. When the parts of nature are seen in their proper relations, 'they appear as sounds of one voice, impulses of one eternal intelligence'.[29] Guided by this view of nature, he made discoveries that contradicted it, but that won him glory. And glory, as we have seen from the outset, was what he sought.

Davy was concerned, both within himself and in pleading his cause before society, to establish a proper sense of the nobility of the scientific enterprise. He was fond of quoting Bacon. In 1808 he told an audience that Bacon had said that 'The introduction of noble discoveries seems to hold by far the most excellent place among all human actions; and this was the judgment of antiquity which attributed <u>divine</u> honours to inventors, but conferred only <u>heroical</u> honours on those who deserved well of their country in civil affairs. And whoever rightly considers, will find this a judicious custom.....' Davy believed that everything grand and dignified had arisen from the union of science with religion.[30] Through the semi-autobiographical mouthpiece of the Unknown, the hero of his <u>Consolations in Travel</u>, he assured his readers that 'there never has been a higher source of honour or distinction than that connected with advances in science'. To understand the operations of nature and their utility for man, 'to bring the lightning from the clouds and make it subservient to our experiments' - in such activities lay glory, honour, even sublimity. Like Bacon, Davy felt that light was superior to fruit, that understanding was superior to application - but genius, he believed, consisted in the perpetuation of individual existence through ideas that in their application transformed society.[31] Thus light and fruit were interdependent, and both contributed to glory. In this scheme, Romantic and utilitarian ideals reinforced one another.

Davy wanted the immortality that was the due of scientific genius. He was not, however, immune from more immediate ambitions. 'It is not that honours are worth having', He observed, 'but it is painful not to have them'. It was, after all, only just that civilized society should recognize the merits of those who had most contributed to its prosperity. 'In reality', Davy explained, 'the origin, as well as the progress, and improvement of civil society is founded in mechanical and chemical inventions'. Even in his early years, he took a liberally but not exclusively utilitarian view of the sciences, which, he argued, 'ought to be considered as related to man only so far as they are capable of promoting his happiness'. Chemistry deserved well in such a scheme; it was not only conducive to intellectual delights, but it applied to the needs and operations of everyday life which, perfected by science, 'have become the sources of the most refined enjoyments and delicate pleasures of civilized society'. Science, in short, was more than speculation and theory; it was at the heart of progress and civilization.[32]

Davy's own useful contributions included his work in tanning and agricultural chemistry, and his attempts to reduce the corrosion of ships bottoms. But the miner's safety lamp was his greatest practical triumph. Among other tributes, he received a service of plate at a dinner in Newcastle in 1817. Davy's speech of acceptance expressed his satisfaction at the knowledge that his work had contributed to 'arts,... manufactures, commerce, and national wealth. To learn this from such practical authority,' he continued, ' is the highest gratification to a person whose ardent desire has always been to apply science to purposes of utility'. He descanted upon the importance of science to the sources of wealth and power in the state; and concluded by stressing the circumstance that his invention of the safety lamp was the fruit of the pursuit of proper scientific method. In glory, in utility, in pleasure, and in rewards, there should be no divorce between pure and applied science.[33]

Balance was crucial - Davy had a profound contempt for those who would debase science to mere application, and who failed to perceive the splendour of the discovery of a new law. The fabric of law that unified nature was what the chemical philosopher sought, and the dignity of science was independent of its applications.[34] But those applications, resting upon scientific discovery, were not to be despised. Light gave rise to fruit, and both contributed to pleasure and glory.

Certainly Davy's own pleasure was much enhanced by the renewed recognition that his discovery won for him. Sir Joseph Banks wrote cordially to him that, although his researches on the safety lamp were intrinsically less brilliant than those on the alkali metals, they would be of greater service to the Royal Society and to the public image of science. John Playfair, who had courted Jane Apreece, generously wrote that 'it may fairly be said that there is hardly in the whole compass of art or science a single invention of which one would rather be the author... This is exactly such a case as we should choose to place before Bacon, were he to revisit the earth, in order to give him... an idea of the advancement which philosophy has made..[35] In view of the rage for empiricist Baconianism, this was a compliment indeed. So too was the baronetcy that the safety lamp won for Davy. His career was punctuated by honours, and this, combined with his humble origins, made him a perfect illustration of Samuel Smiles <u>Self Help</u>. 'What I am', said Davy, 'I have made myself. I say this without vanity, and in pure simplicity of heart'.[36] Elsewhere, he tells us what he is: poet, philosopher, sage, benefactor of mankind, and genius. Having considered him under the three last categories, it is time to return to the first two.

    He had early determined to pursue a career in science rather than in poetry, making a clear distinction between the poetic and the scientific apprehension of nature, following a different path from the Romantics while admired by them. Real philosophers - pure scientists - had often through their researches conferred material benefits upon mankind, while offering delight and enrichment to the intellect. It was this double function that marked the superiority of science to poetry. Poetry exalted the mind, but had no absolute utility. Scientific pursuits reached to the heavens in their 'sublime speculations', while belonging in their application to the earth. In a complete reversal of the judgment of Coleridge, Davy compared great poets unfavourably with great natural philosophers. 'At that time, when Bacon created a new world of intellect, and Shakespeare a new world of imagination, it is not a question to me which has produced the greatest effect upon the progress of society — Shakespeare or Bacon, Milton or Newton'. Works of poetic imagination 'resemble monstrous flowers, brilliant and odorous, but affording no materials of re-production'.[37]

The message was clear. Scientific discovery was glorious, and the achievements of scientific imagination were for Davy higher than those of poetic imagination precisely because the former bore fruit while the latter were brilliant but materially barren. Davy may have provided Romantic poets with their prime English example of scientific genius and creativity, but except for a period of youthful mutual sympathetic admiration, Davy did not reciprocate their sentiments. Coleridge once described Shakespeare's writings as nature realized in poetry, and Davy's chemistry as poetry realized in nature. Davy would have denied that there was such a symmetry between poetry and science. He was no mere utilitarian; but his ambitious quest for glory has its utilitarian as well as Romantic aspect. His last book, <u>Consolations in Travel</u>, epitomizes the blend of dignity, utility, permanence, and consonance with the tenets of reason and religion, that characterized Davy's vision of science. And the utterances of the Unknown constitute Davy's own <u>apologia</u> for a life spent in science and society.

NOTES

1. T.H. Levere, 'Coleridge, Chemistry, and the Philosophy of Nature', <u>Studies in Romanticism</u>, 16 (1977), 349-379. H.G. Soderbaum (ed.), <u>Jac. Berzelius Bref.</u>, 6 vols + 3 suppl., Uppsala, 1912-32, vol.2, pp.35-59. Harold Hartley, <u>Humphry Davy</u>, London, 1966, p.148.
2. E.L. Griggs (ed.), <u>Collected Letters of Samuel Taylor Coleridge</u>, 6 vols., Oxford, 1956-71, vol.5, p.309. S.T. Coleridge, <u>The Friend</u>, ed. B. Rooke, 2 vols., London and Princeton, 1969, vol.1, p.471; <u>Philosophical Lectures</u>, ed. K. Coburn, London, 1949, p.25.
3. <u>Works</u>, vol.1, p.13; Hartley, op.cit. (1), p.12.
4. <u>Works</u>, vol.1. pp.59-60.

5. *Fragmentary Remains*, p.34. J.Z. Fullmer, 'The Poetry of Humphry Davy', *Chymia*, 6 (1960), 102. R. Southey (ed.), *The Annual Anthology*, 2 vols., Bristol, 1799-1800, vol.1, 93-99, 120-125, 172-176, 179-180, 281-286; vol.2, 293-296.
6. Reprinted in Paris, *Life*, vol.1, pp.25-29.
7. H. Davy, *Consolations in Travel, or the Last Days of a Philosopher*, 1st ed., London, 1830; 5th ed., London, 1851, p.238. *Works*, vol.1, p.212; *Consolations*, 1851, p.244.
8. *Works*, vol.1, p.147. Morris Berman, *Social Change and Scientific Organization: The Royal Institution*, 1799-1844, London and Ithaca, 1978.
9. R. Sharrock, 'The chemist and the poet: Sir Humphry Davy and the preface to the *Lyrical Ballads*', *Notes and Records of the Royal Society of London*, 17 (1964), 57.
10. S.T. Coleridge, *Poetical Works*, ed. E.H. Coleridge, London, 1973, p.595. *Fragmentary Remains*, p.33.
11. *Works*, vol.1, pp.62, 60. *Consolations*, 1851, p.18. *Works*, vol.1, pp.24-25, 186.
12. *Fragmentary Remains*, p.14.
13. *Works*, vol.1, pp.66-67. Cf. T.H. Levere, 'S.T. Coleridge: A Poet's View of Science', *Annals of Science*, 35 (1978), 33-44; T. McFarland, *Coleridge and the Pantheist Tradition*, Oxford, 1969; D.M. Knight, 'The physical sciences and the Romantic movement', *History of Science*, 9 (1970), 54-75; D.M. Knight, 'The Scientist

as Sage', *Studies in Romanticism*, 6 (1967), 65-88.
14. Lecture of 1811, based on lecture of 1805, in Works, vol.8, pp.200, 347.
15. B. Gower, 'Speculation in Physics: The History and Practice of *Naturphilosophie*', *Studies in History and Philosophy of Science*, 3 (1973), 301-356.
16. Levere, op.cit. (1). pp.349-379; Levere, *Affinity and Matter: Elements of Chemical Philosophy 1800-1865*, Oxford, 1971, p.33 (R.I. Davy Ms, n.d. but ca. 1808). D.M. Knight, *The Transcendental Part of Chemistry*, Folkestone, 1978, chap.4.
17. *Fragmentary Remains*, p.13.
18. Berman, op.cit. (8).
19. J. Colmer, *Coleridge Critic of Society*, Oxford, 1959, reprinted 1967. K. Coburn (ed.), *The Notebooks of Samuel Taylor Coleridge*, vols. 1-3 of 5, London, 1957-73, vol.2, entry 1855.
20. Bristol City Archives, Ms 32688/31, 22 June 1801.
21. Griggs, op.cit. (2), vol.2, p.768.
22. Pace Berman, op.cit. (8), especially chap.2; my indebtedness to Berman is none the less considerable and obvious.
23. Hartley, op.cit. (1), *passim*.
24. Coleridge, The *Friend*, vol.1, pp.94, 471. Levere, *Affinity and Matter*, chap.4.

25. W. Wetzels, 'Aspects of Natural Science in German Romanticism', Studies in Romanticism, 10 (1971), 44-59 (53).
26. See note (16) above, and especially Studies in Romanticism, 16 (1977), 361. S.T. Coleridge, note on flyleaf of G. Berkeley, Siris, 2nd ed. Dublin and London, 1744, in Beinecke Rare Book Library, Yale University.
27. Levere, Affinity and Matter, p.46.
28. H. Davy, 'The Bakerian lecture, on some chemical agencies of electricity', Phil. Trans., 97 (1807), 1-56; 'The Bakerian lecture, on some new phenomena of chemical changes produced by electricity, particularly the decomposition of the fixed alkalies...', Phil. Trans., 98 (1808). 1-44. Both papers use Lavoisier's concept of an element while correcting Lavoisier's table of elements. Griggs, op.cit. (2), vol.3, pp.38, 41. Berzelius, Traité de chimie, trans. Jourdain & Esslinger, 8 vols., Paris. Henry Brougham, Edinburgh Review, 11 (1808), 390-398, 394-401, 483-490.
29. R.I. Davy Ms. 1, quoted in Levere, Affinity and Matter, pp.66-67.
30. Fragmentary Remains, pp.59, 164.
31. Consolations, 1851, pp.238, 258; Works, vol.1, p.62.

32. <u>Works</u>, vol.1, p.69;   vol.2, p.315;   vol.8, p.87.
33. <u>Works</u>, vol.1, pp.207-208.
34. <u>Fragmentary Remains</u>, p.58.
35. Banks to Davy, 30 October 1815, in <u>Fragmentary Remains</u>, pp.208-209. <u>Works</u>, vol.1, p.202.
36. S. Smiles, <u>Self Help</u>, 1st ed. 1859;   London, 1908, p.14.
37. <u>Consolations</u>, 1851, pp.257-259. <u>Works</u>, vol.1, pp.147, 212. Levere, op.cit. (13), 42-44.

Humphry Davy, Reformer

J.Z. Fullmer

'Reformer' is an ambiguous tag. A reformer may refashion, remake or reshape a thing; a reformer may also attempt to redirect or change the philosophy guiding an institution or practice, to redress grievances. Humphry Davy was an active reformer in both senses of the term. Beginning in 1797 and throughout his career he aimed to remake, to refashion, to re-form chemistry. Davy's other major reforming effort, his attempt to redirect institutional practices within the scientific community, cannot be dated so precisely. By 1820, however, when he assumed the Presidency of the Royal Society his aims as institutional reformer had crystallized. He sought to redirect the Society and to obliterate the inequities accumulated during Sir Joseph Banks's long tenure in the chair.

Davy's efforts to refashion the conceptualizations at the heart of chemistry were in large measure effective. His attempts and his accomplishments mirrored the resolution of some of the conceptual dilemmas plaguing Regency chemistry specifically, and natural philosophy generally. Moreover, his endeavour through the agency of the Royal Society to reshape the practices in, and the recognized composition of the scientific community coincided with the perceptions and aspiration of many of his scientist colleagues. Davy lived when winds of reform stirred the English political climate. Changes in the condition of humankind, propelled by spiralling industrialization and heightened by wars, raised the expectations of large segments of the populace. Not long after Davy's death in 1829, the ruling classes could no longer ignore the clamour for 'one man, one vote'. Scientists had no such galvanizing slogans, but they too wanted changes; many of them shared the philosophical position from which the political reformers operated. Davy's attempts to articulate and meet felt needs of the scientific community mirrored the state of affairs within and without that community. Thus a study of Davy as reformer becomes more than a biographical exercise: what this study ultimately depicts is the fluid state of the conceptual base of natural philosophy, and some of the prevailing sociological tensions within the scientific community as industrial society took shape.[1]

Davy's efforts to change the conceptual foundation of chemistry began late in 1797. They were inspired by his reading of the one chemical text available to him, Lavoisier's <u>Traité élémentaire de chimie</u>.[2] Davy detected in the treatise ideas far too close for his intellectual comfort to the earlier phlogistonist ideas of Stahl. Not only did he perceive that some of Lavoisier's assumptions and conclusions would not bear experimental scrutiny, but he also saw that Lavoisier worked in a tradition alien to British natural philosophy. That tradition he had learned from the one other chemical work available to him in Penzance, William Nicholson's two volume <u>Dictionary of Chemistry, Exhibiting the present State of the Theory ... its Application to Natural Philosophy, the Processes of Manufacture... and numerous other Arts</u>.[3] Because from time to time Davy bent necessity and to expedience it appears that he either interrupted his pursuit of reform, or was dilatory. In actuality he was so single-minded that by about 1812 he had achieved a substantial conceptual transformation. Moreover, in 1826 his sixth and final Bakerian lecture to the Royal Society revealed how truly fruitful his reforms were, for his new conceptualization had pushed and led him to a still more acute understanding of the natural world.

In 1799 Dr. Thomas Beddoes, his mentor and guide at the Pneumatic Institution in Bristol published Davy's first scientific papers: 'An essay on heat, light and the combinations of light' and 'An essay on the generation of phosoxygen, or oxygen gas: and on the causes of the colours of organic beings'.[4] In them Davy argued that the prime task for chemistry was to show what were simple bodies and what compounded. Lavoisier in the Traité had published a list of simple substances; 'lumière' (light) led the list, followed by 'calorique' (the substance of heat). Davy announced that the latter ought to be removed from the list because heat was not a substance; heat was motion. Yet, despite his discomfiture with this basic Lavoisierian postulate, Davy showed in these two papers that he was not totally immune to its seductions, for he elected to retain light as a substance entering into chemical reactions. Accordingly he urged the transformation of chemical nomenclature; to indicate that the substance of ordinary combustions was generally comb-ined with varying amounts of light, it should be called 'phosoxygen' rather than 'oxygen', the term Lavoisier coined. Retaining light as an elemental substance was compatible with Davy's Newtonianism, but his insistence revealed something too of his own psychology, for him chemical reality ultimately depended on experimental demonstration. Ordinary combustions do indeed assault the senses with heat and light. Davy, already at eighteen a dedicated experimentalist, found the mere rearrangement of bare corpuscles too frail a mechanism to support the vivid sensual phenomena he had so often observed.

    Davy's overt and covert criticism of Lavoisier came to the scientific community with the imprimatur of Dr. Beddoes, one of Lavoisier's earliest and strongest British champions. Such sponsorship guaranteed Davy's papers serious scrutiny. Reactions came quickly.[5] While critics noted that Davy's insistence that heat was motion was contrary to received opinion, that insistence was not singled out for special animus. Responsible critics objected chiefly that Davy's experimental results were not robust enough to support his conclusions. "H.L." in the <u>London Medical Review</u>[6] and Dr. John Ferriar writing anonymously in the <u>Monthly Review</u> were agreed. Dr. Ferriar complained:

> To us the experiments do not convey demonstration: they are of so delicate a nature, and express such a very slight alteration of temperature, that a few trials of them would furnish no satisfactory evidence; and, even admitting their accuracy, create difficulties rather than furnish explanations: for, as Mr. Davy asserts the materiality of light, he still adds an unanalyzed fluid to the list of chemical subjects.[7]

"H.L." further charged Davy with being far too mechanistic when viewing living systems. That criticism bothered Davy not one whit. What stung him then, when he was nineteen, and what would sting him throughout his life was the charge that he had failed as an experimenter. His notebooks show his anger and hurt; there he railed at the reviewers, rejecting them as 'closet chemists', as non-experimentalists blindly adhering to the 'bible of Stahl and Lavoisier'.[8] Still, a letter Davy wrote to his quondam patron, Davies Giddy, dated before the reviews appeared, shows that Davy was himself unhappy with his experiments, and for a very interesting reason: he had come to believe the nature of heat was demonstrable by logic alone. He used an experimental array, he told Giddy, when he was 'an infant in speculation'.[9] He began to draft a new essay, 'Observations on the Philosophy of Heat and Light', to demonstrate without recourse to experiment that heat was insubstantial. Yet the uncompleted draft shows the strong pull that observational data held for him. Despite his professed commitment to metaphysical argument, the essay disintegrated into disjointed paragraphs recalling experimentally won data.[10]

Davy's distrust of the basic Lavoisierian tenets can best be gauged in his first truly chemical paper, 'Experiments and observations in the silex composing the epidermis or external bark, and contained in the parts of certain vegetables'.[11] His biographer and brother, John Davy, extravagantly admired the paper, reprinting a large portion of it;[12] earlier his continental contemporaries, Swiss, French and German, spread his opinions through their translations.[13]

Upon learning that bonnet canes gave off luminous sparks when struck together Davy tried to discover the cause of the sparking. In a series of chastely severe tests he was able to demonstrate that the sparking ability of canes, reeds and grasses depended on their epidermal flint, or 'silex' (the Lavoisier-sanctioned term for silica). His experimental conclusions drawn, Davy, dutiful disciple of Dr. Beddoes, hoped that chemistry might provide 'further inferences to the speculator on organized nature'. Flint, 'entering into the composition of these hollow vegetables, may be considered analogous to the bones of animals', Davy continued. Then he raised a chemist's problem, expressed in chemist's language. The presence of silex in grasses, he said, 'will probably enable us to determine whether silex be a simple or a compound substance'. Were a grass to be grown in a silex-free environment, he suggested, it would be possible to 'discover whether it would compose silex, or substitute for it another earth'. Davy obviously chafed at the lack of chemical means to resolve the problem of simplicity or compounding. To isolate the silex he had used chemistry's most powerful agents: the blow torch; strong, hot, oxidising acids; strong alkalies. Silica emerged from all these treatments an unscathed, white flocculent enigma. So despairing of the efficacy of conventional agents was Davy that he indicated his willingness to move to another kind of experimentation, to exploit the plant world because 'the numerous complex attractions of organic beings, resulting from their variety of composition, are continually producing changes which the art of the chemist is unable to imitate'. The chemist was at the end of his tether, for 'at present ⌐he⌐ can extend his power no further by the simple attractions and repulsive motions of inorganic matter'.[14] That condensed jeremiad put the matter exactly. Chemistry was a matter of simple attractive and repulsive motions; experiments with available agents had been pushed to their limits.

It might be assumed that when Davy read in Nicholson's *Journal* of Volta's experiments with the pile he leapt to its use to solve his prime chemical problem; after all, following Volta's description of the pile was Nicholson and Carlisle's demonstration that the pile could decompose water into its elements.[15] That assumption would however be wrong. Davy characteristically required a short period, sometimes a few days, more often a few weeks, before he took an experimental action in response to what he had read in the literature. His first public notice of the pile appeared in an 'Appendix' to his book on nitrous oxide. He wrote the final pages on 5 June 1800; thus, he noticed the pile as soon as he had read of it, but before he had performed any experiments. Still his reading was perceptive, for he said that a reaction he had already studied, the conversion of nitrous gas to nitrous oxide in the presence of moist zinc, copper or tin in contact with mercury was doubtless another example of the kind of phenomenon discussed by Volta and by Carlisle.[16]

His own experiments with the pile began very early in July. From September on, readers of Nicholson's <u>Journal</u> had monthly bulletins about their course. Since Davy's papers are relentlessly autobiographical, it is possible to follow the development of his ideas almost day-by-day. His first report showed that the problem of determining which substances were simple and which compounded was overarching; he suggested that perhaps 'nascent hydrogen [achieved by pile decomposition] will become a powerful and accurate instrument of analysis'.[17] Nonetheless, his attention had subtly shifted. About the pile two major questions can be asked: how does it work? what can be done with the curious electrical fluid (or fluids) it appears to produce? Davy answered each in turn. Even though the answer to a third question: what is the mysterious Voltaic fluid? was intimately bound to answers to the other two, he deliberately chose not to confront it.

First he attempted to discover how the pile worked. In October Davy's readers learned that carbon functioned in the pile as well as metals did.[18] In November he reverted to earlier observations, to ask if it was possible to say something about the causes of galvanic phenomena. Could the power of the pile be increased? He concluded that chemical changes connected with the oxidation of the zinc in the pile were 'somehow the cause of the electrical effect it produces'.[19] Davy anguished that he had to write 'somehow'; not only did he italicize the word, but that same month he sent Nicholson a supplementary note,[20] always a sure sign of his uneasiness in the face of unfinished business. In the note he attempted to expand his ideas and especially to fix the meaning of the 'somehow' to which honesty had impelled him. While he still discussed pile construction, he showed that he was also seeking a precise chemical explanation for its behaviour; he referred explicitly to the 'peculiar affinities' among substances, thereby inviting the reader to recall the importance of affinity theory to chemical studies. By December Davy approached enunciating a quantitative law of pile behaviour: 'one quantity of chemical action generates in the galvanic series ... an influence capable of increasing all analogous actions, and of generating new, similar actions'.[21] Moreover, the problem of what was simple and what compounded was still central, for Davy asked his readers if 'the new phenomena of galvanism [did not] authorize us to hope that at no very distant time [we will] behold even ... [the] gases undergoing novel changes, and existing in new and unknown forms?'

After February 1801 the bulletins in Nicholson's *Journal* ceased; in March Davy moved from Bristol to London to take up work in the house of the Royal Institution. His researches continued, but now he published them in the *Journals of the Royal Institution* and discussed them in his public lectures. Galvanism was the topic for his first series, beginning on April 25, strong indication of the importance of the topic to his audience and to him. In June, Count Rumford presented to the Royal Society Davy's first paper to that body '... Some galvanic combinations ... analogous to the new galvanic apparatus of Mr. Volta'. Here Davy elegantly summarized his previously published novel findings.[22] Collecting his conclusions had permitted him to emphasize in new ways the connections between galvanic electricity and chemical changes.

Davy very early emphasized that although the Voltaic pile had been discovered elsewhere, and that universally it 'awakened the love of investigation', what understanding there was of how it functioned chiefly reflected the efforts of British workers. They had amassed evidence which provided a general elucidation of the connection between chemical changes and galvanic electricity.[23] His insistence on the magnitude and importance of the British contribution paralleled his convictions about chemistry. For Davy the true tradition of natural philosophy stemmed from Newton; moreover a Newton-derived chemical tradition stemmed specifically from the work of Joseph Black. Contributions from the French, that is, from Lavoisier and his followers, Davy regarded almost as a detour or roadblock delaying chemistry on its course. Among the many reasons for his insistence on Englishness and on Britishness, two present themselves as compelling. Setting contemporary events aside, when Davy looked back from a conceptual point of view, he saw the British contributions to be the decisive ones. Moreover, his own sense of citizenship, always prominent, was heightened by contemporary political events. As the nineteenth century opened, peace was in jeopardy. The lull created by the treaty of Amiens proved temporary. Times called for solidarity on all fronts, including intellectual ones, against a threatening enemy. Finally, Davy's patriotic invocation reveals him at his most subtle as a fund raiser. The Royal Institution needed from its patrons not only their good will but their contributions. Were Davy to have a newer and stronger battery, which he indeed wanted, money to buy it could come from one source, his audience. Discreetly he implied that the noble tradition of 'British science' should be continued. In his lectures Davy proved deft at stirring the hearts of his hearers, at engaging them intellectually, and especially at arousing those impulses that opened pocket books.

Still, despite Davy's patriotic claims, the

state of chemistry left much to be desired. In 1802 he apologized to his audience, saying that chemistry 'as yet is not furnished with a precise and beautiful theory'; the natural philosopher hoped 'by ... experiments to interrogate nature with power ... as a master, active with his own instruments'. He recognized the pile as 'a new influence', capable of 'generating from combinations of dead matter effects which were formerly occasioned only by animal organs'. To know which substances were elemental was the most important task, for undecompounded substances 'are the <u>sensible</u> agents of chemistry; before we can examine the nature of compound bodies, or particular phenomena of composition or decomposition, it is necessary that we should be acquainted with their characteristic properties, and with certain of the modes in which they are procured'.[24] It was a refrain of which he never tired.

Davy mingled his complaints about the present state of affairs with hopes for the future in his lectures, just as he mingled his chemical and physiological observations with electrical ones. Soon, however, he abandoned the physiological considerations. Between 1802 and late 1806, when Davy appeared engrossed in practical affairs of special concern to his supporters - tanning, geology, agriculture - and he was not experimentally active with the pile, shreds of evidence repeatedly surface to show that electrical and chemical queries were never far from his mind. Certainly the literature kept the subject alive, since his contemporaries continued to experiment along electrical lines. Many of them, often far less talented than Davy, crowded the journal pages with reports of untidy pile experiments. They touted their ambiguous results as illuminating the question of the nature of the galvanic fluid and as providing insight to pile behaviour. Read consecutively, such reports in <u>Philosophical Magazine</u> and Nicholson's <u>Journal</u> for the period 1802-1806 sound almost as if they had been written before the turn of the century, even though the authors were using an 1800 invention, the Voltaic pile.[25]

    Davy must have wearied of this kind of reading. In 1806, when experimental interpretation had muddied to opacity, he moved, finally, to settle matters. His first Bakerian lecture to the Royal Society, 'On some chemical agencies of electricity' simultaneously put an end to the blather and opened the way for new experiments. Davy spelled out a fruitful way to view questions of pile behaviour, and, in so doing, coined the word 'electrochemical' in what was essentially a lesson in experimental hygiene. A sensitive reader could learn what clean experiments were, and how to think cleanly about the results. The conceptual base was 'electrochemical'. Moreover, Davy stated clearly how he thought the pile worked. As translations, abstracts and reports of the lecture circulated, his contemporaries both at home and abroad became privy to the insights Davy had been formulating since July of 1800.

If Davy's first Bakerian took an initial and giant step to solve the problem of how the working of the pile might best be understood, there remained, still, the other question - what could be done with it? Sporadic demonstrations of its use had already appeared. Nicholson and Carlisle in 1800 had shown its usefulness in decomposing water; Cruickshank's experiments revealed how the pile might be used to remove a metallic constituent from a solution.[27] Davy's second Bakerian, delivered 19 November 1807, 'On some new phenomena of chemical changes produced by electricity...' addressed the question.[28] His answer proved dazzling, and, once his results were accepted as valid, the conceptualization on which they were based gained a firm foothold. According to a surviving notebook, on October 6 Davy began the series of experiments 'On polarization' he detailed in this lecture.[29] Against the power of a galvanic battery made from 100 plates of 6 inches he tried the following substances by placing them on glass plates and touching them with platinum wires connected to the battery: dry oxalic acid, succinic acid, tartaric acid, soap, water, ammonium carbonate, potassium nitrate, sulfuric acid, and a candle flame. Potassium nitrate produced spectacular results.

Edmund Davy, his laboratory assistant, reported that when Davy saw the material fuse and then liberate small granules resembling quicksilver which burst with explosive violence, he joyously danced around the laboratory. It took quite a while before he was able to settle down to continue the series.[30] He repeated the experiment with potassium nitrate about two weeks later and devised a new one, using soda. The soda similarly decomposed, and almost as spectacularly. While it would be pleasant to dwell on these experiments, and his reasons for choosing these materials to test, to see how he went about interpreting his results, and to see how he argued for the simplicity of the substances he isolated (and soon christened potassium and sodium, names independent of the conceptualization which gave them birth), there is time only to ask why he indulged in a dance as he watched the forming material. The reasons were ample: Davy had increased the number of simple substances; simultaneously he had shown that he had to hand the means to get at what was to him the basic chemical problem; in addition, getting at the basic chemical problem would enable him to show the heresy of the 'bible of Lavoisier'. Davy's arabesques and fandangos celebrated experimental proof for his conceptual reforms.

His experiments, of course, did not stop. By the time of the next Bakerian, 15 December 1808, '...some new analytical researches on the nature of certain bodies...,' Davy had added to his list of newly won simple substances barium, strontium and magnesium; shortly afterwards he indicated that glucinium (beryllium) and aluminium also existed, although he had not been able to isolate them.[31] He had, in addition, begun to tackle the problem of determining the nature of phosphorous, sulfur, carbon and nitrogen. If his subsequent papers demonstrated anything, they showed how limited his razzle-dazzle results would be.[32] One might dwell for a very long time on the intricacies of his later attempts, on the ingenuity of his experiments and on the ambiguity of his results, just as he did. One point must be made: his experiments were logically conceived, an expression of his aim to penetrate to the true nature of chemical substances. Davy's dissatisfaction at his inability to tear apart phosphorous, sulfur, carbon and nitrogen was reflected in the extent of his attack, and by the fact that he sent to the Royal Society a long supplement to his third Bakerian lecture.[33] Viewed with the clarity of hindsight, it is possible to say that Davy's 1809 conceptualization was not yet adequate to explain the answers the real world made to the kinds of questions he asked. Ultimately he exploited his failed experiments to remove that inadequacy.

These developments, it might be argued, scarcely represent true conceptual 'reform.' Viewed doctrinally ' the bible of Lavoisier' was still intact. Yet, Davy's fifth Bakerian lecture, delivered on 15 November 1810, 'On some of the combinations of oxymuriatic gas and oxygene...' revealed that collapse was imminent.[34] Sir Humphry ensured it in a paper he sent to the Royal Society to be read on February 13, 1814, while he was abroad.[35] He left the paper 'An account of some new experiments on the fluoric compounds...' as a possible candidate for yet another Bakerian lecture, but the Fellows, impatient of his stream of Bakerians, declined to so honour it. Perhaps some regretted their decision, for at the close of this brilliant paper Davy demonstrated unequivocally that chlorine was a simple body. His discoveries continued. Subsequent events in France made it possible for him to expand his attack on 'the bible', for, in addition to chlorine and the corrosive and elusive fluorine, he had iodine to discuss.[36] There were, he said, at least <u>four</u> supporters of combustion. Lavoisier had argued for only one. That Davy chose to couch his arguments in these terms - that is, to speak of numbers of supporters for combustion - showed that his aim was to reform the Lavoisierian conceptualization.[37]

Several scholars have commented on Davy's relative invisibility in chemical history: no hypothesis, no law, no element, no fundamental unit remains as his eponymous memorial. Certainly during his lifetime his visibility was great; in the Victorian period both Bowdlerized and Grangerized, his life and work were made to serve as a paradigm for aspiring poor boys.[38] However, as the century wore on even that ghostly emanation faded from view. Davy's subsequent invisibility arose partly from his own actions, and partly because the changes he wrought were so fundamental that it began to seem as if that was the way chemistry had always been. Davy's insistence that the meretricious doctrines of Lavoisier be removed from chemical thinking in effect returned chemical conceptualization to an older tradition. His insistence that names of new elements be without conceptual implications contributed further to his relative invisibility. Thus, his changes in nomenclature obscured the reformed concept-ualization from which they sprang, whereas 'oxygen', the acid-former, stands always as a reminder of Lavoisier's beliefs. Yet that slighted nomenclative reform remains as one of the reasons we celebrate him today. Were Davy's chemical reforms his sole achieve-ment, our celebrations would still be proper, but there was, of course, more to come: the miner's lamp, the works on the nature of flames, the principles of electrochemical corrosion, and the like.

Despite this impressive list it would not be fair to claim that Davy limited himself solely to chemistry, or solely to chemical technology. The quiet reforms he instigated beginning in 1820 within the scientific community have also been overlooked, obscured by the pyrotechnics of events after his death. In Davy's lifetime the professional status of the members of the scientific community emerged as a serious problem. Davy, to be sure, had done well enough as he pursued his chosen work. If his efforts had not brought him great wealth, he was comfortably situated, even without the 'crucible money' acquired through his marriage.[39] More important, his chemical and technological efforts produced for him a gratifying measure of respect and of fame. Yet clearly more support was needed, if not for himself - and it must be remembered that Davy was fundamentally selfless - then for his colleagues. At the close of the Regency, the pursuit of natural philosophy was not yet recognized as a profession. In 1821, for example, Chief Justice Robert Dallas ruled in the Court of Common Pleas that in the eyes of the law chemists were no more professional than were mechanics; they were not on a par with medical doctors or lawyers. Justice Dallas's decision reflected contemporary opinion, largely determined by social and class perceptions.[40] Of these invidious distinctions Davy was certainly aware.

If natural philosophers and chemists were not yet regarded as professionals by some segments of the society, one place to begin to make changes was in the Royal Society, the recognized 'official' voice of the scientific community. Since 1778 its President had been Sir Joseph Banks. At the beginning of his long tenure in the chair Banks presided over the Society, but toward the end of the Regency it is probably fair to say that Banks 'reigned.'

Whenever Banks's precarious health took a turn for the worse, speculation grew about his successor, speculation on which Banks himself was happy to contribute. Like many autocrats, he had come to regard the Society and its Presidency as his special creature. He offered the Chair to various people at various times under various conditions, only to withdraw his offer soon after it was made, sometimes creating embarrassing situations for those he had temporarily anointed.[41]

In 1820 Banks's health took a dramatic turn for the worse; in May he thought he might resign, but he changed his mind. Banks died in office on 19 June, and when word reached Sir Humphry, who was travelling on the Continent, he turned homeward to see what should be done about the matter. Earlier Davy had written to W.T. Brande, his successor at the Royal Institution, that he thought the subject of the Presidency almost a 'national one'; he appeared cool to the prospect of occupying the chair himself.[42] Now however his interest quickened, and he lost little time launching his campaign. The <u>Philosophical Magazine</u> for July announced that Davy was almost certain to become the new P.R.S.[43] Major and minor skirmishes occurred after that announcement, but by August opposition had been overcome.[44] About 640 Fellows were eligible to vote on St.Andrew's Day in 1820. One hundred and sixty votes were actually cast, of which Davy received all but the thirteen which went to Lord Colchester.

Once seated on the raised platform in Somerset House, the Royal mace before him, wearing the tricorn of court dress, but not a powdered wig or ruffles, and flanked by the two Secretaries, Davy was in a position to redeem his campaign promises.[45] Davy became President of the Royal Society by promising reform, reform in the sense of redressing grievances and correcting inequalities. His program had the over-all aim of redirecting the Society so that it would more truly reflect the composition and interests of the English scientific community, as well as become more responsive to the needs of that community.

Davy's reforms can be grouped under five general heads: new Fellows were to be elected into the society for reasons that were at once more stringent and more liberal, for they were to be demonstrably practising scientists, chosen from a far wider segment of society than in Banks's time. Secondly, 'sister' societies, whether devoted to scientific specialities or to regional interests, were to be encouraged. Thirdly, practitioners of science in areas alienated by Banks's policies, particularly mathematicians, astronomers, and geologists, were to be repeatedly reassured that their work made valuable contributions to the community. Fourthly, the Society would publicly encourage individual scientists, especially those who previously pursued their self-appointed tasks at great personal cost. Finally, and perhaps most important of all, stronger ties were to be forged between the scientific community and the government; the Royal Society was to be the chief agency for that connection.

Narratives about attempts at reform have a certain sameness; that describing Davy's attempts is no exception. For some, reforms can never come quickly enough, because corrections of abuse may often be too late for those who have suffered; for others, exhausted by battle, or for tempermental hotheaded zealots, no reform can be drastic enough. A third group, characterized usually by an apparent Olympian detachment and a 'go-slow' attitude, frequently attempt to preserve a status-quo. Davy encountered every category of reaction. His reform campaign was weakened by attack from those who thought he was doing too little, and from those who thought he was attempting far too much too quickly. Moreover, beginning late in 1823 Davy was himself weakened by the first of a series of cerebral accidents whose cumulative effect was to cause him to resign the chair in 1827.[46]

Davy first attempted to broaden the Society's base. Even though it has been duly recorded, the import of one of his changes has never been discussed. Banks had instituted Sunday evening parties at his Soho town house for Fellows, their friends and distinguished guests. Davy continued the practise with one modification; he switched the day of the party from Sunday to Saturday. On the surface the change may appear scarcely worth mentioning, but by the switch Davy encouraged and made possible participation by those scientists whose non-conforming religious scruples prevented them from attending to secular matters on the Sabbath. As Davy was well aware, this group included some of the most vigorous and enterprising members of the scientific community; it was, moreover, the group from which, in future, many new Fellows were to be recruited. These evening parties continued until 1826, when Davy changed house. Then the Council, at Davy's request, moved the parties to coincide with the meeting days of the Society, and authorized the use of the Library in the Society's rooms for them. While the Council appropriated money for candles to light the room, they agreed that the President would continue to defray the cost of the food served. Davy had also hoped to include women in these evening parties, but his colleagues refused.[47] Davy's desire to welcome both women and the non-conformist segment of the scientific community testifies to his sympathetic connection to a special group of reformers, and to his recognition of the importance of informal communications in scientific circles.

In addition to altering the time for quasi-social gatherings, Davy sought also to change the pattern of Fellowship. In 1823 his committee to remake the Statutes made its work public.[48] Subsequent critics complained that the committee had not restricted the number of Fellows to be elected annually. The revised statutes did reduce the allowable number of Foreign Members and did curtail the privileges of those members of the Peerage who sought 'instant' Fellowship. Even though there were no new requirements for Fellowship, Davy attempted to interpret strictly the existing requirements; had all the Fellows adhered to strict interpretation, the number of new Fellows would have been reduced. On the basis of the revision, new Foreign Members were to have to their credit 'scientific discoveries and attainments', rather than meeting the older requirement for 'literary endowments'. Davy took that requirement seriously, and as expressive of intent for the selection of Fellows. In 1823 reform sentiments ran high, for the number of elected Fellows fell to sixteen, the lowest number admitted in a decade. There is other evidence of Davy's attempts to improve the quality of the Fellowship. On 11 December 1823, a certificate on behalf of Sir Francis Shuckburgh, Baronet, of Shuckburgh Park, Warwick, was introduced. Shuckburgh's sponsors included the Earl of Winchelsea, H.T. Colebrooke, Walter Hartig and Arthur de Capell Brooke, names hardly guaranteed to strike resounding chords in the hearts of the scientific community. They shared an interest in foreign travel, in the East India Company, and in Tory politics. As the statutes required, Shuckburgh's certificate was displayed for ten weeks. Sometime during those weeks Davy wrote across the top of the certificate 'No qualifications mentioned', and across the bottom, 'This certificate ought not to have been presented, there being no qualifications mentioned. H.D.' Clearly he behaved arrogantly, or angrily, or else he mistrusted his colleagues reforming zeal. Davy could hardly have been pleased with the vote, for the certificate also bears the endorsement 'Ballotted for & elected the 11 March 1824'.[49] In that year twenty-four new Fellows were admitted, an indication that after a brilliant start impetus for reform waned.

Another area where Davy wanted changes concerned the connection between the Royal Society, as the voice of the scientific community, and the government. His most compelling arguments were both patriotic and utilitarian. The scientific Fellows with their special knowledge would prove useful to the government, he said, but it is obvious that he also hoped that the government could be made more useful to the scientific community. Davy's arguments, publicly aired, found special emphasis in his first Presidential address.[50] Although at pains to remind his audience that utility was not the be-all and end-all of science, he also asked the Fellows to look to 'practical applications', not forgetting 'the dignity of ⌐their⌐ pursuit, the noblest end of which is to exalt the powers of the human mind, and to increase the sphere of intellectual enjoyment, by enlarging our views of nature, and of the power, wisdom, and goodness of the Author of nature'. He asked the Fellows if they might not labour together to 'gain what are perhaps the noblest objects of ambition - acquisitions which may be useful to our fellow creatures. Let it not be said', he concluded, 'that at a period when our empire was at its highest pitch of greatness, the sciences began to decline'. These sentiments resurfaced, but not until 1830, and then from the pen of Charles Babbage.[51]

The twin emphases on usefulness and on patriotic duty, however, hindered Davy's attempts to create the connections with government he so ardently sought. Bank's entrée to the Crown's influence was guaranteed through his courtier relationship with George III. Times had changed when Davy became President; he could not create the same sort of alliance with George IV. Davy inclined to Whig views, and enjoyed Holland House connections. At first the Whigs assumed George IV favorable to their reforming causes, but they found him a continual disappointment, for the very best he ever offered was coalition government. Moreover, George IV could hardly have been pleased when he heard that his unfortunate wife, Caroline, had made an abortive attempt to annex both Sir Humphry and Lady Davy to her entourage.[52] Nonetheless, Davy had to try to gain the sympathy and support of the Crown. He used his Vice President, Davies [Giddy] Gilbert, for liaison with Commons and to continue the consulting role with the Boards of Admiralty and Longitude.[53] Davy forged his own pipelines to Castlereagh and to Liverpool, but above all he cultivated Robert Peel, His Majesty's Principal Secretary. Through Peel's good offices Davy received for the Royal Society additional space in Somerset House, and funds to establish the Royal Medals. Proper bestowal of the medals permitted the Society (and, indirectly, the Crown) to recognize special achievements which might otherwise go uncelebrated. Davy demonstrated, too, the Society's growing muscle by leading the Council to veto the first charter for the newly forming Royal Society of Literature. Especially he showed that endorsement by the Royal Society helped to speed financial help from the Crown to scientific workers. By Davy's lights these were small accomplishments. He wanted a more clearly defined role for the Royal Society in the affairs of the British Museum; he wanted the recently founded Royal Zoological Society, in whose creation he had played a seminal part, to assume responsibility for assisting farmers and fishermen to improve their stock; he wanted, in sum, the narrow road between science and government to be broadened into a two-way boulevard.

At the end of his life it seemed that the gap between what he desired and what he had achieved was very great. In the detached despair that marked his final days, while he mourned that gap, he overlooked his outstanding accomplishment. By his actions and by his words Davy made it possible for the Fellows to discuss reform openly; he had changed the character of the Presidency by pointing to areas where reform might well begin and he started the Society down the path. In short, Davy made reform a respectable topic within the scientific community.

Davy's initiation of institutional reform had far-reaching consequences: sister societies sprang up, without weakening the Royal Society; the Fellows were increasingly recruited from the ranks of practising scientists; slowly the government sought and heeded the advice of the scientific community; even more slowly, the government encouraged that community and came to its aid. Yet, activist President that Davy was, the mantle of reformer appears to have been denied him. Subsequent events have led historians to claim that the reforms within the scientific community coincided with political reforms, or possibly with the publication of Babbage's <u>Decline of Science in England</u>. Still, Babbage's specific pleas were not those of a pioneer; he strongly echoed Davy's earlier efforts.

Davy's reform of chemical conceptualization has likewise escaped wide notice, partly because his success was so absolute. Even as he created a new sub-discipline, electrochemistry, he shaped the central core of chemistry, the parent discipline. Historians, if they comment at all, generally perceive the 'chemical revolution' as a series of incidents surrounding Lavoisier.[54] Considering the complexity of the history of chemistry, and its intimate connection with medicine, with the myriad technological arts and with geology, that perception is surprising. Close reading of historical record makes it even more so. As we have seen, Davy regarded the basic conceptualizations of Lavoisier as wrong, based on a tradition inimical to correct chemical thinking. If all his contemporaries did not immediately share his view, many did; the rest were soon won over by his spectacular successes and by their own subsequent achievements once they adopted his informing insights. When Davy died in Geneva in 1829, he was sadly crippled by afflictions that kept him from experimenting; Lavoisier died by the guillotine, all his powers intact. Both men were justly mourned, and justly, the accomplishments of both should be celebrated. If Lavoisier gave chemistry clarity and an elegant intellectual panache, Davy brought to chemistry elegance of experiment, a reformer's zeal, and a refusal to blink at the conceptual consequences of experimental results.

NOTES

This paper was presented at the Humphry Davy Bicentenary Symposium, the Royal Institution, 6-9 December 1978. My participation was made possible by grants from the College of Humanities and the Graduate School, Ohio State University, from the ACLS-NEH international Travel Fund, and from the Royal Society, through the agency of the Royal Institution. I am grateful to all.

1. The data which this paper summarizes is so massive that it required violence of compression, first, of Davy's accomplishments, and second, of the sources on which the argument is based. The analysis depends on a close reading of Davy's published works, of his notebooks and commonplace books preserved in the Archives of the Royal Institution, and of his letters, the originals of which are preserved in libraries all over the world. It depends, too, on study of the administrative documents for both the Royal Institution and the Royal Society, and on diaries and notebooks of his contemporaries, both published and unpublished. In addition, it exploits, again by close reading, all of the scientific journals published during Davy's lifetime and after, in England, Scotland, Ireland, Switzerland, France, Germany, Italy, the low countries, Russia, and the United States.

Study of official documents preserved in the Library of the House of Lords, in Guildhall, in the Parliamentary Papers and in the Board of Admiralty supplemented this material. To supply a picture of the intellectual ambience in which Davy worked, three contemporary encyclopedias were analyzed page by page, including the 35-million word <u>Cyclopaedia</u> edited by Abraham Rees, along with the intellectual and popular magazines and newspapers of his day. In short, this discussion is based on the same materials which lie at the heart of my Davy biography, already underway.

J.Z. Fullmer, <u>Sir Humphry Davy's Published Works</u>, Cambridge, Mass., 1969, provides complete bibliographical citations for all of Davy's known publications. It will be cited as <u>SHDPW</u>, followed by year and number of the entry.

2. Antoine Lavoisier, <u>Traité élémentaire de chimie, présenté dans un ordre nouveau et d'après les découvertes modernes</u>, Paris, 1789, 2 vols. There were several editions; Davy read the work in French, but which edition is not known.

3. William Nicholson, <u>A dictionary of chemistry, exhibiting the present state of the theory and practise of that science, its applications to natural philosophy, the processes of manufactures, and numerous other arts</u> ..., London, 1795, 2 vols.

4. SHDPW, 1799:6 and 1799:7. Works, vol.2, pp.3-88, 89-122.
5. SHDPW, 1799:6R and 1799:7A.
6. London Medical Review, 1 (1794), 384-394.
7. Monthly Review, 30 (1799), 63-65.
8. R.I. Davy Ms, notebook 20b.
9. H. Davy to Davies Giddy, Clifton, 22 February 1799, quoted in Paris, Life, vol.1, pp.76-79. The phrase 'an infant in speculation' has often been wrenched from context, and nearly as often misunderstood; the most recent example of such distortion is Anne Treneer, The Mercurial Chemist, London, 1963, p.37.
10. R.I. Davy Ms, notebook 20b.
11. SHDPW, 1799:8. Works, vol.2, pp.133-138.
12. Memoirs, vol.1, pp.84-89.
13. SHDPW, 1799:8T and 1799:8C.
14. Works, vol.2, p.137.
15. W. Nicholson and A. Carlisle, Journal of Natural Philosophy, Chemistry and the Arts (Nicholson's Journal), 4 (1800), 179-187.
16. SHDPW, 1800:2. Works, vol.3, pp.337-339.
17. SHDPW, 1800:3; 1800:4; 1800:6; 1800:7. Works, vol.2, p.150.
18. SHDPW, 1800:4. Works, vol.2, pp.150-154.
19. SHDPW, 1800:5. Works, vol.2, pp.155-163.
20. SHDPW, 1800:6. Works, vol.2, pp.163-165.
21. SHDPW, 1800:7. Works, vol.2, pp.166-181. SHDPW, 1801:1. Works, vol.2, pp.181-182.

22. SHDPW, 1801:2. Works, vol.2, 182-188. See also SHDPW, 1801:5; 1802:8 and 1802:15. Works, vol.2, pp.209-213, 214-219.
23. SHDPW, 1801:5. Works, vol.2, pp.188-209.
24. SHDPW, 1802:1; 1802:4. Works, vol.2, pp.307-326, 327-434.
25. J.R. Partington, A History of Chemistry, London, 1964, vol.4, p.41, notes 8-15 review some of the literature.
26. SHDPW, 1806:3. Works, vol.5, pp.1-56.
27. Nicholson's Journal, 4 (1800), 187-191.
28. SHDPW, 1807:6. Works, vol.5, pp.57-101.
29. R.I. Davy Ms, Laboratory notebook. The notebook is described as the 'public' laboratory notebook.
30. Ms memoir by Edmund Davy, R.I. Davy Ms.
31. SHDPW, 1808:6. Works, vol.5, pp.140-224.
32. For example, SHDPW, 1812:4. Works, vol.5, pp.358-390.
33. SHDPW, 1809:1. Works, vol.5, pp.205-224.
34. SHDPW, 1810:16. Works, vol.5, pp.312-348. This paper should be read in conjunction with the earlier 'Researches on the oxymuriatic acid, its nature and combinations ...' read to the Royal Society, 12 July 1810. SHDPW, 1810:14. Works, vol.5, pp.284-311.
35. SHDPW, 1814:2. Works, vol.5, pp.425-436.

36. J.Z. Fullmer, 'Humphry Davy and the Iodine Priority Dispute: further documentary evidence', Ambix, 22 (1975), 39-51.
37. Letter to Dr. John Davy, Florence, 18 March 1814. Memoirs, vol.1, pp.481-483.
38. J.Z. Fullmer, 'Davy's Biographers: Notes on Scientific Biography', Science, 155 (1967), 285-291.
39. 'Crucible money' is Sydney Smith's phrase. Letter to Lady Holland, 16 November 1816, in Nowell C. Smith (ed.), Letters of Sydney Smith, 2 vols., Oxford, 1953, vol.1, p.268.
40. J.Z. Fullmer, 'Sugar Technology, Chemistry and the Law in Early Nineteenth Century England', Technology and Culture, 21 (1980), 1-28.
41. A.C. Todd, Beyond the Blaze, Truro, 1967, pp.212-217.
42. Letter to W.T. Brande, Paris, 20 May 1820. W.T. Brande, A Manual of Chemistry, London, 1836, 4th ed., pp.99-100.
43. The Philosophical Magazine, 56 (1820), 58.
44. L.F. Gilbert, 'The Election to the Presidency of the Royal Society in 1820', Notes and Records of the Royal Society, 11 (1955), 256.
45. Letter from Leonard (sic) Horner to Dr. Marcet, Edinburgh, 10 April 1821. Katherine M. Lyell (ed.), Memoir of Leonhard Horner, 2 vols., London, 1890, vol.1, pp.191-192.

46. Letter to Lady Davy, Laybach, 1 September /1828/, R.I. Davy Ms., 'I have been used so ill by the public when I have labored most to serve them & injured my body & mind in exertions for their good (Witness safety lamp copper bottoms Royal Society)...'
47. All of these matters emerge from the Minutes of Council and from Committee Reports, Royal Society Archives.
48. The working copy of the revised statutes is preserved in the Royal Society Library.
49. Certificate on behalf of the Fellowship of Sir Francis Shuckburgh in the Certificate Books, Royal Society Archives.
50. <u>SHDPW</u>, 1820:3. <u>Works</u>, vol.7, pp.5-15.
51. Charles Babbage, <u>Reflections on the decline of science in England and on some of its causes</u>, London, 1830.
52. The letter is preserved in the R.I. Davy Ms.
53. Todd, op.cit. (41), pp.221-229.
54. I.B. Cohen 'The Eighteenth-Century Origins of the Concept of Scientific Revolution', <u>Journal of the History of Ideas</u>, 37 (1976), 257-288, pointed out that the idea of a Lavoisierian 'chemical revolution' was fixed in 1890 when Marcelin Berthelot published <u>La révolution chimique: Lavoisier</u>.

Davy and Gay-Lussac: Competition and Contrast
Maurice Crosland

Davy was an important figure not only in British science but also on the European scene. Of particular significance is his relation with scientists in France where the new science of chemistry had recently come into being through the efforts of Lavoisier and his colleagues.[1] Davy's work was published in French journals,[2] and it is well known that he spent several weeks in Paris at the height of the Napoleonic wars. This has sometimes been used by historians of science to argue that 'the sciences were never at war'[3] (a quotation from Jenner) but we might oppose this with a quotation from Davy who drafted a lecture in which there appears the claim that 'there is one spirit of enterprise, vigour, and conquest in science, arts and arms'.[4] A study of some of Davy's work reveals some of the rivalry that existed in intellectual matters between Britain and France but the story would not be complete unless we considered also the personal dimension.

Davy's reputation has depended on many factors personal, institutional and national. It has depended for a large part of the nineteenth century on the devotion of his scientific brother who, of course, not only wrote a full biographical study but edited and published Humphry Davy's scientific works in nine volumes. His reputation has also been fostered by the Royal Institution, with which he was so closely associated, and also by the Royal Society, of which he was president. He was seen as representing the best of English science at a time when war emphasized national differences. There were of course British naval and military heroes in the Napoleonic wars and it was understandable that some should have seen in Davy the scientific hero.

The position of Gay-Lussac is rather different. Unlike Davy he did not stand out among his contemporaries as a lone hero. This was partly because some of the work in which he rivalled Davy was carried out in collaboration with Thenard, but it is even more because in France, or at least in Paris, there was a sizeable scientific community. It is therefore more natural to see Gay-Lussac as one of a number of distinguished French scientists of the time rather than a lone genius. When he died France was not particularly looking for heroes and, although there were the usual brief commemorations, there was no life of Gay-Lussac published. This had to wait until the twentieth century when a local historian wrote a pious commemoration called 'the noble and moving life of Gay-Lussac'. Nor was Gay-Lussac favoured with an editor who would bring together his many published papers and Gay-Lussac was even less a scientist who wrote books than Davy. The publication of a scientist's best work in periodicals, although serving a useful purpose at the time, is likely to bury achievement rather than display it to later generations. All this will help to explain why Gay-Lussac is much more of an unknown than Davy. Indeed his very name provides a stumbling block to some Englishmen and Americans who refer to him as GUY-Lussac. Yet he was the leading French chemist in the generation after Lavoisier, the generation of Davy.

I should say a few words about Gay-Lussac. Born in December 1778, the same month and the same year as Davy, Gay-Lussac was born into a middle class family in central France. With the Revolution Gay-Lussac's father lost his job because of a remote connection with the crown. Gay-Lussac was sent to Paris to complete his education and was fortunate enough to be admitted to the newly established Ecole Polytechnique, where he had an excellent training in mathematics, pure and applied, physics and chemistry. It was not until his final year, however, that he showed any special preference for chemistry. This was when he was working on problems of bleaching with chlorine with Berthollet. Even then Gay-Lussac's first published work, on the thermal expansion of gases, enabling him to enunciate what is ofted mistakenly called 'Charles Law', would usually be classified as 'physics'. Gay-Lussac's early training qualified him to teach physics at the Faculty of Science but his interest in the subject matter of physics dwindled and he was to make his name almost entirely in the field of chemistry.

Gay-Lussac became a répétiteur in chemistry at the Ecole Polytechnique being promoted to professor of chemistry at the death of Fourcroy in 1809. He was later to be professor of chemistry at the Museum of Natural History, a job which provided him in the 1830s and 1840s with a comfortable house not far from central Paris. Some of his lectures were published, but without his permission. As a member of the Academy of Sciences Gay-Lussac became a leading figure in the French scientific establishment and was twice elected president of the Academy. Although Gay-Lussac made a reputation for himself in pure science, his law of combining volumes of gases, his work on the halogens, boron and cyanogen, he turned increasingly to applied science and his name is given to the tower used in the manufacture of sulphuric acid by the lead chamber process. He developed titrimetric analysis to a point where it could be widely used in industry. His method of estimation of silver as silver chloride revolutionised assaying and provided substantial savings for the French government. The Gay-Lussac centesimal scale for alcoholic liquors was recognised as a vast improvement on previous methods of estimation and an international committee has recently recommended that the scale should be accepted universally to replace such antiquated pre-scientific concepts as 'degrees proof'.

But this is not a paper on Gay-Lussac. My purpose is rather to say something about some of the similarities and differences between Davy and Gay-Lussac and in my treatment there are no heroes and no villains, just men, prompted by the usual fears and passions and with strong interests in chemistry. Of course one was an Englishman and one was a Frenchman and the two countries were at war almost continuously from 1793 to 1815. For Davy France was probably first the country of Lavoisier but it was also a nation which had killed its king and had given general support to the Revolution. It was latterly under Bonaparte a country which was trying to dominate the whole of Western Europe. It was therefore difficult in the opening years of the nineteenth century for an Englishman to feel neutral towards things French and it was doubly difficult for an ambitious young chemist who had to come to terms with Lavoisier's system. Davy showed this in his 1799 paper in which he tried to introduce 'phosoxygen' to make a substantial modification of Lavoisier's theory.[5]

Davy's research on nitrous oxide published in 1800,[6] and Gay-Lussac's research on the thermal expansion of gases of 1802,[7] clearly made known the work of the Englishman to the Frenchman and vice-versa. It was not until 1807, however, that they were to be engaged on similar research. Once this competition started - since one can hardly speak of it in terms other than competition - it continued on similar lines for at least seven years. Much important work was done by the chemists on both sides of the Channel during this period and there can be no doubt that much of it was done in conscious rivalry, each side studying carefully all reports on the work of the other. Sometimes areas of scientific research are regarded as private property and, if this is accepted, then the question of poaching arises. Both Davy and Gay-Lussac had certain proprietorial instincts but both published their work and so placed it in the public domain, where the concept of poaching seems inappropriate.

But even this does not explain fully how Gay-Lussac came to be studying Davy's research. In two cases, the electrolysis of potash and soda, and the investigation of iodine, Gay-Lussac was first involved not as a private individual but as a member of the First Class of the National Institute, which had an important judicial function inherited from the eighteenth-century Academy of Sciences, and was quite different from the traditions of science in Britain.

The Institute awarded prizes for outstanding work regardless of nationality and Davy's Bakerian Lecture of 1806 published in the Philosophical

Transactions had been carefully studied by a committee of the First Class (with Gay-Lussac as secretary) as a candidate for a prize of 3,000f on electricity.[8] Ironically no sooner had the committee decided to recommend Davy for the prize when the news came of his decomposition of the alkalis, surely research even more deserving of a prize than the Bakerian Lecture. When the award of the prizes was announced at a public meeting of the Institute in January 1809 Gay-Lussac was able to refer also to the decomposition of the alkalis. But we cannot pretend that Gay-Lussac or indeed any other Academician was devoted single-mindedly and disinterestedly to the function of the Institute as a judging body. Gay-Lussac was an ambitious young scientist and in collaboration with Thenard he investigated the new field with excitement and not without some hope of personal achievement. Their first achievement was to prepare potassium and sodium by chemical reduction in amounts large enough to investigate accurately the physical and chemical properties of the new elements, something Davy had been unable to do with the tiny amounts produced by electrolysis. Gay-Lussac also made substantial use of potassium as a reagent; for example in the isolation of boron. Here again there was great competition between the chemists, Davy reading eagerly the progress report published by Gay-Lussac and Thenard in one of the issues of the *Moniteur* of May 1808. The first published claim to the isolation of the new element in a pure state was published by the French chemists in the <u>Moniteur</u> of 15 and 16 November 1808, whereas Davy was not to make a similar claim until December. Davy, however, was happy to give credit to Gay-Lussac and Thenard for their preparation of pure hydrofluoric acid and 'fluoboric gas' (BF_3) in 1809 but once this work was published it was used quite properly as a basis for further research by John Davy.

Although the isolation of new compounds is always interesting, probably Gay-Lussac derived more intellectual satisfaction from an understanding of chemical composition particularly by quantitative analysis. He used potassium to analyse various gases and the information obtained by the decomposition of nitric oxide provided data to confirm his law of combining volumes of gases. He was surprised that so-called 'oxymuriatic acid gas' was not decomposed when passed over strongly heated charcoal and suggested that it might not contain oxygen after all. Berthollet persuaded him to publish this in the Arcueil <u>Mémoires</u> of 1809 as no more than a hypothesis, and it was Davy who very properly receives credit for recognising the gas unambiguously as an element which he called 'chlorine' (1810).

The most famous example of rivalry between Davy and Gay-Lussac is the case of iodine, a rivalry which has been misunderstood since it involved much more than national rivalry. It is also an incident which has developed a mythology based on the claim of John Ayrton Paris[9] that the French chemists had long had the opportunity to examine the substance but that its recognition as a new element iodine was entirely the work of Davy, bringing a superior genius to the problem. But Gay-Lussac too had a claim to the discovery although his involvement had been misconstrued. He first examined the black substance (discovered in 1811 by Courtois) not as a private individual, a potential rival to Davy, but as a member of the First Class of the Institute. Courtois had handed the mysterious new substance on to the aspiring provincial chemist Clément, who had examined it in collaboration with Desormes. Clément had his eye on a vacancy in the First Class for the position of correspondent in the chemistry section and he hoped to direct favourable attention to himself by presenting a memoir in November 1813, just before the election.[10] Clément's memoir on the unknown substance was pedestrian but its importance lies in the questions it left unanswered about the new substance and the fact that memoirs submitted to the First Class were normally given to referees for their opinion. The experts chosen by the Academy to look at the memoir were: Gay-Lussac and Thenard. Hence Gay-Lussac's first introduction to iodine was in an official capacity.

November 1813 happened to be the time of Davy's

visit to Paris and he had been welcomed most warmly by young men who were outside the scientific establishment, particularly Ampère, not yet a member of the Institute. It was Ampère and his friends Clément and Desormes who introduced Davy to the new substance a few days before Clément read his memoir to the Institute. Clément, possibly disgruntled as an unsuccessful competitor in a prize competition of the Institute the previous year, was hoping to win the approval of the famous English chemist by showing him this new substance which produced a spectacular violet vapour on heating. However, by also submitting the same research to the Institute within a few days he unwittingly set the two old rivals on the same trail and in clear competition. J.A. Paris's insinuation about the French chemists is probably justified in relation to Clément and Desormes. It was not justified in relation to Gay-Lussac and Thenard.

Having carried out their referee's duties, Gay-Lussac and Thenard could not resist taking the work further on their own account. Clément and Desormes had said that the new substance formed muriatic (i.e. hydrochloric) acid with hydrogen and Davy's first opinion was similarly that it was 'a compound of chlorine and an unknown body'.[11] The first public announcement of further research came on Monday 6 December when Gay-Lussac presented his research to the First Class of the Institute. He thought the new substance was probably a new element which he proposed to call _iode_. The memoir was published in the _Moniteur_ of 12 December. Davy hardly had the same rights of access to what was after all a French government publication, but he decided to present his own research verbally to the First Class at its next meeting of 13 December. Some doubt remains as to when Davy actually completed the memoir he presented that day, but he dated it 11 December, i.e. the day before Gay-Lussac's publication. Further evidence on the problem of priority is provided by a recently discovered memorandum in one of Gay-Lussac's laboratory notebooks,[12] but with the passage of time the whole question of priority seems less important if not trivial. What seems clear is that both Davy and Gay-Lussac independently took the study of _iode_ or iodine much further than Clément. Each may have independently recognised it as an element although Gay-Lussac (on home ground) achieved the first publication. If he had the first word on the subject he also in a sense had the last, since he continued his research on the element and its compounds for several months after Davy had left Paris. The result was the 'Memoir on iodine' published in August 1814, its 155 pages filling an entire issue of the _Annales de chimie_. Even John Davy was generous in his praise of this memoir[13] and Ostwald described it as 'one of the first and one of the best monographs of all time on a single element and its most important compounds'.[14]

Gay-Lussac's research on iodine involved a detailed study of iodic acid and hydriodic acid and prompted him to divide acids into two classes: the traditional acids containing oxygen and a new class which he called 'hydracids'. Indeed a whole section of his classic memoir on iodine was devoted to the question of acidity. This was the last issue which was to exercise both Gay-Lussac and Davy although, as this was a question of interpretation and articulation of a theory rather than discovering a substance, there was less of the old spirit of rivalry in establishing priority.[15] The competition over the years 1807-1814 was probably generally beneficial to the participants and certainly to science. Each side could correct or complement the work of the other. In the case of Davy the fact that others were working in the same field probably had the effect of concentrating his attention on a problem long enough to bring a piece of research to completion. Yet it has been justly said[16] that another effect of the French competition was to hurry his work so that some of it was not as good as it might otherwise have been. Certainly one of the effects of obsession with priority is premature publication and it is interesting to compare and contrast the style of publication of the two great chemists. In fact there are differences which transcend temporary problems of priority and reflect difference of personality and the different conditions under which natural knowledge was pursued in the two countries.

It was characteristic of Gay-Lussac that in nearly every memoir he should stress the provisional nature of his conclusions. He continually avoided the responsibility of deciding between alternative hypotheses and in the case of chlorine he lost credit for understanding that it was an element by putting this forward as no more than a possibility. Gay-Lussac reveals himself as something of a pre-positivist in his rejection of speculation and the fact that he was often contented simply to collect new data.

Although Davy was usually more confident in his approach than his French rival, there were obviously many cases when he too was unsure of his ground. It is worth looking at the ways in which he then safe-guarded his position. His approach provides a good contract with the style of Gay-Lussac. The latter would often sit on the fence and achieve security at the expense of some possible triumphs. Davy preferred to make more positive claims, often supporting simultaneously several alternative possibilities. He was prone to speculation and he would later claim credit for predictions which had subsequently been confirmed by experimental evidence. One example of this is his Bakerian Lecture of 1807, which he began with the statement that he was now able to substantiate his ideas on the power of electricity to isolate elements.[17] This, he claimed, had been his conclusion to the Bakerian Lecture which he had delivered in 1806. If, however, we look for confirmation of this claim we find that the Bakerian Lecture of 1806 concludes with a rather long and diffuse passage.[18] Although the idea mentioned is present, it is no more than one of a number of speculations with which Davy had entertained his audience. With hindsight Davy was able to rescue this speculation, but nothing is said about several other curious ideas mentioned in the same lecture. In the same way even to-day, Davy tends to be remembered for his (correct) identification of chlorine as an element, while his (incorrect) views that nitrogen, sulphur, phosphorus and carbon were really compounds[19] have conveniently been forgotten by all but Davy specialists.

Davy boldly scattered seeds broadcast and, when plants of various kinds grew up, he was happy to harvest the best of them. If I may continue the metaphor for Gay-Lussac, it would be to suggest that he sowed seeds more carefully but failed to gather the best harvest. Davy may sometimes have been too bold but the Frenchman was not bold enough. Davy believed that he was capable of important new insights. Gay-Lussac was more modest by temperament and lacked Davy's self-confidence. He felt that he could not afford to be wrong and therefore continually refused to commit himself.

Some explanation must be offered of Gay-Lussac's

reluctance to make innovatory claims. Part of the answer lies in his education and the authoritarian nature of French science. Gay-Lussac's training at the Ecole Polytechnic and at Arcueil had impressed on him the orthodoxy of the French scientific establishment and particularly the views of Berthollet and Laplace. Yet in most of his scientific research there was no question of him contradicting these views. What Gay-Lussac really feared was the responsibility of innovation. He could work within the framework of established ideas without assuming any great burden. But making a claim involves commitment and responsibility and Gay-Lussac may well have felt this responsibility all the more keenly as a member of the small professional scientific community based on Paris. If he had been an isolated individual, perhaps an obscure figure in the provinces of France, he could well have afforded the risk of a mistake. Such a person would have nothing to lose and much to gain by attracting the attention of the famous scientists in the capital. Also it could be argued that Gay-Lussac was working within a French tradition which respected good experimental work but tended to distrust new theories. He therefore knew that he was safe in reporting his laboratory work, so carefully planned and executed, and that he would be respected for this alone.

The great exception to this general characterisation of Gay-Lussac's work is his deep commitment to establishing general laws of nature.[20] Had he been a man who never went beyond laboratory data he would not have been a great scientist. His reputation as a scientist is not based simply on his work on the study of particular substances such as potassium and iodine. It rests rather on his study of the relations between various physical and chemical phenomena and on the statement of several fundamental scientific laws. Gay-Lussac's faith in order within nature was sufficiently strong for him to overcome his normal reluctance to go beyond the data.

A further difference between the two men lay in the Frenchman's professionalism. Despite Davy's early association with the Royal Institution, he apparently felt it a relief to abandon his position as professor of chemistry to live the life of a gentleman. Davy aspired to a superior social position, which in England at that time was incompatible with salaried employment. Berzelius thought that Davy could have been one of the greatest geniuses in the whole history of chemistry - if only he had had to study the science systematically in his youth. He was, however, largely self-taught and Berzelius concludes that he had contributed only a few brilliant fragments to chemistry.[21] Gay-Lussac on the other hand, had undergone a specialised scientific education at the Ecole Polytechnique. He gained a certain rigour and discipline lacking in the more dilettante approach of the English scientist. But he lost the freedom to explore any area of the natural world from any point of view.

Although Gay-Lussac and Davy both gave scientific lectures, there were important differences between their positions and also between their audiences. Davy's audiences at the Royal Institution were drawn from the upper classes, people who could afford to pay the necessary subscription. The Royal Institution audience included many ladies, whose aim was amusement as much as instruction. Gay-Lussac's teaching was more serious and, if he occasionally carried out demonstration experiments, it was as a basic pedagogic aid rather than a striving for the spectacular. His audience was either to a highly selected academic group, as at the Ecole Polytechnique, or at an elementary level at the Faculty of Science. Gay-Lussac was therefore fulfilling an academic rather than a social role. Gay-Lussac, as a graduate of the Ecole Polytechnique, a professor in a state system and a member of a sizeable scientific community, was a professional scientist. It is hard to consider Davy as a professional scientist. He would more aptly be considered as a professional lecturer, owing a special allegiance to his employers and his public and only secondarily to his scientific colleagues. Whereas Davy saw moral values in science, Gay-Lussac may be taken to represent the common modern view of an amoral value-free science.

In order to emphasise the difference of approach of Davy and Gay-Lussac, which went beyond institutional differences in Britain and France, I am going to use the terms 'romantic' and 'classical' despite the way in which these words have been abused and the well-known difficulty of providing definitions.[22] I would not wish to push the romantic view of Davy too far but I will consider him from this viewpoint mainly to highlight certain characteristics of Gay-Lussac. Regardless of whether we accept the romantic image of Davy, our understanding of Gay-Lussac is deepened if we cast him in the classical mould.

Gay-Lussac was primarily interested in order. He wanted a tidy universe and saw it as the scientist's job to recognise this order. He had a certain interest in classification, but the general method he used to impose order was to quantify. Gay-Lussac's two laws of gases are concerned with proportions - the proportion by which a gas expands when it is heated, or the volumetric proportion in which gases like hydrogen and oxygen combine when they are sparked together. (There are no laws named after Davy, and he was not much concerned with correlations.) Gay-Lussac was also concerned with precision. It never quite became an obsession - as in the later case of Regnault - but he was only able to achieve what he did by attention to detail and insistence on exact measurement. Davy did comparatively few quantitative experiments, although of course in the generation after Lavoisier, every chemist was involved to a certain extent in measurement, if only in reporting the quantitative composition of a new chemical compound. Typically Gay-Lussac made an important contribution to the <u>quantitative</u> analysis of organic compounds. One of Davy's embarrassing mistakes, his claim that ammonia contained oxygen, was based on a single quantitative experiment hastily performed. Gay-Lussac, as we have seen, was much more cautious and more patient. If we think of Wordsworth's lines from the <u>Lyrical Ballads</u>:

> One moment now / can bring us more
> Than years of toiling reason

Gay-Lussac's scientific work, as indeed the work of so many modern scientists, could be represented as 'years of toiling reason'.

Davy was very much of an individualist both by temperament and by his position in early nineteenth-century England. Although a Fellow of the Royal Society and an associate of the Royal Institution, he enjoyed a large degree of independence, particularly after his marriage. There were few pressures on him to conform except on the social plane. We have seen him as something of a rebel in orthodox science in his first publication. It would have been a great triumph if he could have shown Lavoisier was wrong. He interpreted his work on the alkalis as a falsification of Lavoisier's oxygen theory of acidity.[23]

By contrast Gay-Lussac did not want to destroy Lavoisier's theory but only to amend it where necessary, as in his work on hydracids. He was influenced above all by his patron Berthollet and, when he discovered his law of combining volumes of gases, he was at pains to explain this as being not incompatible with Berthollet's theory of variable combining proportions. One of the characteristics of French science was its strong specialisation. Research was pursued in depth in limited fields. In Britain, however, there was a very much wider approach to knowledge and for Davy nature was a unity resulting from God's plan of creation. Gay-Lussac did not have a religious outlook. He seems to have had little feeling for the beauty of nature. He represented reason rather than feeling and there are strands of positivism throughout his work. When many of his contemporaries, including Davy, allowed their imaginations to soar over the possible powers of the new electricity, Gay-Lussac showed comparatively little interest in this new field. Whereas Davy has been associated with dynamic chemistry based on forces, Gay-Lussac's work relates more closely to the <u>Chemical Statics</u> of his mentor, Berthollet. Davy's romanticism is clearest in his non-scientific work, but is also present in many of his early papers.

Gay-Lussac's work was certainly a classic in another sense of the term; in the sense in which Ostwald included two of his research papers among his <u>Classics of Science</u>, i.e. it constituted a standard or model. It was also clearly an extension of the work of Berthollet and Lavoisier. Sometimes showing less originality than Davy, as in some of the research on elements, Gay-Lussac's work can be related to a tradition of French physical science. Much of Gay-Lussac's work is characterised by clarity of thought and by completeness - his memoirs on combining volumes of gases and iodine provide two examples of this. Finally, Gay-Lussac's work is characterised by restraint. When his readers would sometimes wish him to make a leap, he is content with a sober exposition of the facts. He is analytical. Gay-Lussac shows a great objectivity. He presented experimental results in tabular form, thus allowing the consistency of his work to be readily checked. His self-effacing modesty may be contrasted with the cult of the ego, more typical of the romantic. For Gay-Lussac chemistry was a discipline, for Davy it was an adventure.

Davy, poet and scientist, had a comparatively short scientific life. He made good use of his imagination in his scientific work. Perhaps if 'romantic' means anything in connection with Davy it has clearest meaning by contrast with his French contemporary.

I have said little about the different ways in which Davy and Gay-Lussac actually carried out experiments beyond the hint that whereas Davy relied on the inspiration of the moment, Gay-Lussac was painstaking in nearly everything he did. Perhaps a better contrast between 'romantic' and the 'classical' in science is to be found in the choice of subject matter. Davy's early researches were concerned with light and electricity, both subjects giving full scope to the imagination. Gay-Lussac's imagination was of a more disciplined kind. He looked for regularities in nature and made his name by the discovery of the laws of gases and by analysis. The other aspect of science where I hope I have succeeded in making a distinction is in the style of reporting, where Davy's exuberance contrasts with Gay-Lussac's caution. In a scientist imagination is a good thing but it must be controlled. Even Humphry Davy's brother said Davy had too much freedom, but on the other hand perhaps Gay-Lussac was too dependent.

Gay-Lussac lived on for some twenty years after Davy's death in 1829, making a number of important contributions particularly to applied science. Some people might wish to say that Davy died prematurely, that, like many a romantic poet, he burned himself out. One would not have expected any major scientific contribution had he lived another 20 years, although he might well have added to his literary reputation. Like Gay-Lussac he became more of an administrator but he was always careful to appear above all as a gentleman. Gay-Lussac was more the technician, with less snobbery and more commitment to science and technology. So science was served in different ways by two men born under the same star but with quite different temperaments and attitudes to science and to society.

NOTES

1. For a recent assessment of the 'chemical revolution' in France see M.P. Crosland, 'Chemistry and the Chemical Revolution', in R. Porter and G. Rousseau (eds.), The Ferment of Knowledge: Changing Perspectives in Scholarship of Eighteenth-Century Science, Cambridge, 1980, pp. 389-416.
2. Particularly the Journal de physique and the Annales de chimie. For a correction of an allegation of censorship of Davy's work in France, see M.P. Crosland, 'Humphry Davy - An Alleged Case of Suppressed Publication', British Journal for the History of Science, 6 (1972-73), 304-10.

3. The title of a book by Gavin de Beer, London, 1960.
4. Lecture 5, 'Electro-chemical science', R.I. Davy Ms, Box 3, folder 2, 1810.
5. H. Davy, 'An Essay on Heat, Light and the Combinations of Light', Works, vol.2, pp.5-86. See also 'An Essay on the Generation of Phosoxygen', ibid., pp.89-116.
6. Researches Chemical and Philosophical, Chiefly concerning Nitrous Oxide, republished as vol.3 of Works.
7. 'Sur la dilatation des gaz et des vapeurs', Annales de chimie, 43 (1802), 137-175. Translated in Nicholson's Journal, 3 (1802), 207-216, 257-267.
8. The commission was appointed on 28 September 1807. News of Davy's isolation of potassium and sodium in October came to Paris in a letter written by Marcet on 23 November. The decision to award the prize to Davy is recorded in the minutes of the meeting of 7 December: 'Rapport de M. Gay-Lussac au nom de la Commission du Galvanisme', Procès-verbaux des Séances de l'Académie des Sciences, Hendaye, 1910-22, vol.3, pp.626-630.
9. Paris, Life, vol.2, p.22.

10. When the list of candidates was drawn up the following week the names of Clément and Desormes appeared in third and fourth places respectively. Unfortunately for them Humphry Davy was also a candidate and there is some irony in the fact that he was elected by an almost unanimous vote of the First Class.
11. As reported by his assistant Michael Faraday, in H. Bence Jones, The Life and Letters of Faraday, London, 1870, vol.1, p.95.
12. The evidence suggests that the memoir was not completed until Monday, 13 December, i.e. after Gay-Lussac's memoir had been published. For the text see M.P. Crosland, Gay-Lussac, Scientist and Bourgeois, Cambridge, 1978, pp.269-270.
13. Memoirs, vol.1, pp.464-465.
14. Ostwald's Klassiker, No.4, Leipzig, 1889, pp.50-51.
15. A brief discussion of the views of Davy and Gay-Lussac on acidity is given in M.P. Crosland, 'Theories of Acidity in the early Nineteenth Century', Proceedings of the XIIIth International Congress of the History of Science, Moscow, (1971), 67-74.
16. J.R. Partington, A History of Chemistry, London, 1964, vol.4, p.49.
17. Works, vol.5, p.57.
18. Ibid., pp.49-56, see especially p.54.

19. 'An account of some new analytical researches on the nature of certain bodies', Ibid., pp.140-204. Gay-Lussac and Thenard were of course equally wrong in thinking that potassium contained hydrogen.
20. Gay-Lussac speaks of being 'animated with a desire to discover laws', <u>Annales de chimie et de physique</u>, 2 (1816), 130.
21. Berzelius to Wöhler, Stockholm, 3 May 1831, <u>Briefwechsel zwischen Berzelius und F. Wöhler</u>, Leipzig, 1901, vol.1, p.344.
22. As Lovejoy remarked, the term 'romantic' <u>by itself</u> means nothing. I use it only by way of contrast. In 1824 MM. Dupuis and Cotonet tried to collect definitions of romanticism, but after what they described as 'twelve years of suffering', the exercise ended in disillusion and failure; Arthur O. Lovejoy, 'On the Discrimination of Romanticisms', in M.H. Abrams (ed.), <u>English Romantic Poets</u>, 2nd ed., 1974, p.3.
23. M.P. Crosland, 'Lavoisier's oxygen theory of acidity', <u>Isis</u>, 64 (1973), 306-325.

Davy's Chemical Outlook: The Acid Test

John Hedley Brooke

For historians of chemistry the relationship between Davy's achievement and the 'Revolution' of Lavoisier which preceded it has been a subject of considerable interest. Insofar as it is possible to distil a conventional view it would run something like this:

For all his brilliant analysis of the process of combustion, which dealt the death-blow to a Protean phlogiston, Lavoisier committed a basic error in his theory of acids. In choosing to call oxygen 'oxygen' he wished to emphasise its role as a unique acid producer and thereby made the mistake of declaring 'not only that air, but the more pure part of the air enters into the composition of all the acids without exception; and that on this substance their acidity depends ..'.[1] In order for chemistry to recover from this limited and misleading induction, it was necessary to establish at least two distinct propositions that oxygen was not a <u>sine qua non</u> of acidity and that if anything was, it was hydrogen. On this conventional view, Davy earns full marks for showing that there were indeed acids devoid of oxygen, and almost, if not quite, full marks for perceiving the essential role of hydrogen. In a linear history leading from Lavoisier to Liebig and Laurent, Davy stands astride the line with both eyes forward. Thus Sir Harold Hartley wrote that Davy came 'tantalizingly near to the unitary theory of compounds and the hydrogen theory of acids',[2] while an earlier commentator found a 'very significant hint of a future subversion of a traditional doctrine' and found it in Davy's realisation that nitric and sulphuric acids could not be regenerated from nitrates and sulphates without the intervention of bodies containing hydrogen.[3]

Expressed in more sophisticated language this conventional view can be made attractive. There is no doubt that some of Davy's finest achievements did have exciting implications for a theory of acids. Once he had decomposed the fixed alkalies, soda and potash, he could throw out the jibe that 'the principle of acidity of the French nomenclature might now likewise be called the principle of alkalescence'.[4] Once he had concluded his investigations into the properties of chlorine and iodine he was able to relegate oxygen from its unique position: it was no longer alone in supporting combustion and in conferring acidity upon its compounds.[5] Even before his initial study of iodine, Davy had reproached Berzelius for the prominence which the Swedish chemist was still giving to Lavoisier's creation: 'Oxygene with me is not the exclusive neutralising or negative principle. I make others. Chlorine is one perfectly known. The fluoric principle will be another. Others perhaps may be found'.[6] The further corollary of his work on chlorine that the so-called muriatic acid contained only hydrogen and chlorine satisfied Davy that an acid could be an acid without boasting oxygen. It is difficult to imagine a more telling critique of Lavoisier's chemistry. The point that there were acids devoid of oxygen had already featured in Berthollet's critique of Lavoisier's theory,[7] but the merit usually accorded Davy seems to be even more appropriate in the light of the fact that Berthollet's critique was more impressive than pressed. As Homer Le Grand has shown, readers of Berthollet's <u>Essai de statique chimique</u> would have found the objection retracted rather than repeated.[8] Davy was not so pusillanimous. In 1811 he expressed his objection in trenchant form : 'Oxygen ... or the producer of acid is a very improper name for it; for there are very powerful acids that do not contain it, and it exists in the most energetic alkalies. It might be called with more propriety hydrogen, the producer of water..'.[9]

The case for presenting Davy as an effective

reformer of acidity theory is therefore exceptionally strong. Given that he eventually connected the acidity of chloric and iodic acids with the hydrogen they contained,[10] he appears to have been as effective in construction as in criticism. 'It is probable', he wrote, 'that the acid fluid compound of oxygen, chlorine, and water, which M. Gay-Lussac calls chloric acid, owes its acid properties to combined hydrogen ...'.[11] Nor was this proposition lost to view. It was soon publicised by Gay-Lussac himself.[12] If the case for the conventional view required sealing, a stamp of approval could be found in the general consensus among Davy scholars that it was his critique of Lavoisier's chemistry which became the focus of much of his most important work.[13] His inner dialogue with the tenets of the French system has been established beyond doubt[14] and it is well known that it began from the very inception of his career. A notebook from 1799 or 1800 contains the remark that oxygen as the general principle of acidity would seem a 'more extensive' generalisation than the facts admit.[15]

There are, however, several qualifications worth floating because they make the whole subject more interesting and, as I hope to show later, suffused with irony. Some of these qualifications I shall merely summarise because they are of a preliminary nature and may already be found in the literature. Others are worth expounding in more detail because they depend to some degree on differences between manuscript and published versions of two and the same papers.

Of the preliminary qualifications the first would follow from the realisation that Lavoisier was sometimes misrepresented by his critics,[16] that he had never been explicit in proposing oxygen as a <u>sufficient</u> condition for acidity,[17] that he had actually suspected its presence in the alkaline earths[18] - with the consequence, as Gerhardt recognised,[19] that there was a sense in which Davy fulfilled rather than falsified Lavoisier's vision. This would obviously be more true of Davy's decomposition of the alkaline earths than of the fixed alkalies, for Lavoisier appears to have regarded nitrogen as the essential alkalising principle in soda and potash.[20] Nevertheless, even Thomas Thomson, who was quick to seize whatever implications there were in Davy's isolation of sodium and potassium, saw no reason to discount oxygen as a <u>necessary</u> condition for acidity- especially since Davy himself was still regarding fluoric acid as a compound of oxygen and a base analogous to sulphur.[21]

A second qualification concerns the whiggish orientation of the popular view. To streamline the history by searching only for the replacement of an oxygen by a hydrogen theory of acids is to overlook a critical transition period during which any chemist worth his salt, and this was preeminently true of

Davy, was far from clear on issues of both composition and ontology. Though Davy was eventually to claim that muriatic acid was merely a compound of hydrogen and chlorine, the acuteness of the problems is nicely illustrated by the strength of his earlier supposition that oxygen was one of its components. The very paper in which he announced the decomposition of the fixed alkalies contained this sentence : 'the idea of muriatic acid, fluoric acid, and boracic acid containing oxygen, is highly strengthened by these facts'.[22] In the Autumn of 1809 we find him toying with the idea that hydrogen itself might be an oxide[23] - a conjecture which Berzelius was still taking seriously three years later.[24] This kind of confusion in early 19th century chemistry can still come as a shock to those who like to believe that Lavoisier's criterion of the conservation of weight could be used once and for all to decide what was inside what. But, as Robert Siegfried has insisted, the criterion was not always applied when it might have been and in other cases it was impossible to apply.[25] Sometimes it was impossible to obtain a reliable weighing of the product; sometimes it was impossible to combine the supposed constituents of a substance; and always there was the problem that the existence of a recurring minimum weight did not prove that an 'element' was _not_ complex. Accordingly, as late as August 1813, by which time he is usually credited with having won the most notable converts to his view that chlorine does _not_ contain oxygen, we find him writing to Berzelius to say he thinks it probable that it does.[26] True, this was in a context in which Davy insisted on the distinction between what was very probable and what was known, but his admission that chlorine probably contained oxygen was music to his correspondent who lost no opportunity in transposing it for his defence of the traditional doctrine.[27] Berzelius had to acknowledge Davy's inference that muriatic acid could not be a constituent of chlorine, but he was delighted to report that 'it has not escaped the sagacity of Davy that chlorine may contain oxygen...'. The crucial point is that on matters of composition Davy's reforms cannot be reduced to a literally straightforward corrective.

And the same is true on matters of ontology. Indeed Davy's uncertainty on ontological issues was possibly increased rather than decreased by his commitment to a correlation between chemical and electrical states. As Maurice Crosland has emphasised, Davy brought at least three different ontologies to bear on the origins of acidity.[28] In his earliest essays his language was still cast in the mould of principles of acidity, of carriers of properties such as Lavoisier had construed oxygen to be. In later disquisitions it was to the 'peculiar combinations' of the elements that a compound's properties had to be ascribed. And finally, when he could no longer avoid the conclusion that charcoal and diamond were identical in composition,[29] it was to the physical arrangement of particles that Davy turned. His conjectures did not converge on an integrated theory. To distinguish between hints and anticipations, as Gregory is obliged to do,[30] only confirms the artificiality of the whiggish construct.

There is a third preliminary qualification which has been made necessary by Gregory's claim that one can find in Davy a very distinct hint that <u>all</u> acids might be hydrogen acids.[31] The truth is that for Davy to assert that hydrogen made <u>some</u> contribution to acidity in <u>specific</u> cases was by no means the same as to assert that it made an <u>essential</u> contribution in <u>all</u> cases. In the very paper to which Gregory referred, Davy distinctly acknowledged the existence of acids which were simply compounds of oxygene and inflammable bases.[32] This is not to deny the insight which led him to the declaration that 'there are very few of the substances which have been always considered as neutral salts, that really contain the acids and alkalies from which they are formed'.[33] It is, however, to deny that in Davy there is a hydrogen theory of acids.[34] In fact, one of the ironies which I hope to underline is that it was Davy's critics, and Gay-Lussac in particular, who expanded his remarks into a generalisation and did so to facilitate their counter-attack.

Finally among these preliminary qualifications

it is essential to note that the epistemological conclusions which Davy drew from the fact that theories were often in opposition and often ephemeral were such that he could hardly have contemplated the replacement of Lavoisier's generalisation with one comparable in scope and vulnerability. Of the constant opposition of theories he was made acutely aware by his acquaintance with the history of geology.[35] Of the succession of theories and of the dangers of being bound by them he was made acutely aware by the difficulties, by the 'great difficulties', he had experienced 'in conquering the prejudices adopted from the French school' of chemistry.[36] One of his early aphorisms was that preconceived opinions acted like coloured glass[37] and he was to retain the conviction that chemistry was not yet ready for 'general views' concerning the subtle powers of matter.[38] Generalisations were fine when hoisted up by the enemy : one could delight in shooting them down. In this respect it is difficult to deny that Davy's methodological pronouncements reflect his own opportunism. Suspected of 'ensuring that he could not be wrong by putting down in vague terms all possible views of the question'[39] Davy certainly found a thrusting eclecticism the best form of defence.[40]

This brief consideration of strategy will serve as a bridge in taking us towards the more urgent qualifications which spring into view when Davy's immediate objectives are scrutinised. Take, for example, his 1816 paper on the constitution of acids which appeared in the first volume of the <u>Quarterly Journal of Science</u>.[41] His observations on hydrogen, which have so often been seen as pointing to the future, are actually made in a destructive context. His object is not to launch a new theory of his own but to sink once and for all a general theory of acidification which he believes Gay-Lussac still to hold. According to Davy, Gay-Lussac was still using the vocabulary of principles with hydrogen as the <u>alkalising</u> principle. The opportunity to score a point was irresistible. 'If hydrogene be an alkalizing principle', Davy argued, 'it is strange that it should form some of the strongest acids by uniting to bodies not in themselves acid'.[42] One must not read into this critical comment what is not there. Davy derived infinitely more pleasure from expounding arguments than from propounding theories, the fine structure of his own qualifications acting as a persistent irritant to his French opponents.[43]

The critical context in which Davy associated hydrogen with acidity is worth exploring further because the manuscript versions of two of the most important papers suggest that the train of thought which Davy was following was, at least in the first instance, rather different from that which might be inferred from the printed word. In the published versions the train stops short. In the manuscript versions it is allowed to terminate, and in each case the terminus is not a conclusion about acids but a conclusion about the chemical role of water. Now it is perfectly true that to recognise a chemical role for water in the conventional [anhydride plus water] model for the oxacids was an essential prerequisite for a hydrogen theory of acids,[44] but Davy's manuscripts seem to suggest that his remarks about acidity were subservient to the wider objective. 'It is still too much the custom', Davy wrote, 'to consider water as of little importance in combinations yet it not only acts as a solvent but performs the part of a base and we have no right whatever to consider the qualities of anhydrous and hydrated compounds as identical'.[45] This insistence, against Gay-Lussac,[46] on the chemical role of water found an even more revealing expression in the manuscript of the 1816 paper. In both published and manuscript versions the final target was Gay-Lussac's transcription of muriatic acid into hydrochloric. Davy's objection to the new name was elegant : 'Hydrochloric acid would signify chloric acid combined with water, and therefore, according to M. Gay-Lussac's own views, is more applicable to his chloric acid than to muriatic'.[47] In the manuscript version, however, there is this additional and revealing sentence : 'the term hydroacids strictly signifies acids combined with water, and not acids of which one of the constituents is Hydrogene'.[48] Superficially this was a silly slip : if an acid contains water

it must surely contain hydrogen. And yet the very
fact that Davy could write that sentence at all
suggests that he was more preoccupied with the chemistry of water than with a general theory of acids.
Nor is it surprising that he was. More than once
before he had won a chemical argument by showing his
adversaries how their conclusions were vitiated by
the neglect of water. A typical example occurs in
his Commonplace Book : 'M.M. Desormes and Clément had
stated that when the substance /iodine/ was combined
with the metals, metallic oxides could be obtained
from the solutions. I suspected that this depended
upon the presence of moisture or upon oxygene derived
from the air, and experiment justified my suspic-
ion..'.[49] Consequently, when Davy insisted on a
nomenclature that would discriminate between an acid
anhydride and its hydrate he was playing a card that
had won him tricks before.[50]

   The critical context is worth probing further
still because it is clear from his 1816 paper that he
was pursuing two other objectives, both of which
militated against a hydrogen theory. The first was
Davy's quest for a method of classifying the elements,
a quest made all the more urgent, as Ampère recognised,
once an individual element such as oxygen was deprived
of its unique status.[51] Analogies between oxygen,
chlorine and iodine had suggested the value of a
natural classification, Davy himself becoming
increasingly preoccupied with what he called his

'system of analogy'.[52] Thus in the 1816 paper he repeats that 'there is a general chain of resemblance between all the chemical agents'[53] - a chain which, in his <u>Elements of Chemical Philosophy</u>, had included compounds as well as elements.[54] Carbon, boron and silicon were now 'the links between phosphorus and sulphur and the metals', while the basis of 'zircona, glucina, and alumina' will probably form 'a part of the chain between the metals of the alkaline earths and the common metals'.[55] This commitment to chains of resemblance would have made it virtually impossible for Davy to countenance the association of acidity with a single element. In fact it was with specific reference to hydrogen that he chose to anticipate a possible objection : 'hydrogene and azote', he declared, 'stand almost alone; yet hydrogene is connected with the common inflammable bodies by the manner in which it combines with oxygen and chlorine'.[56] No element stood alone in any respect. Deeply concerned with the problems of classification, what Davy was grumbling about in the 1816 paper was that Gay-Lussac was bent on putting the wrong links in the chain. The French chemist had proposed that there was a stronger analogy between chlorine, iodine and sulphur than between the first two and oxygen. Davy disagreed.[57]

The second of the ulterior objectives to militate against a hydrogen theory was Davy's concern to demonstrate once and for all that it was impossible to infer the qualities of a compound from the qualities of its constituents. It was in the 1816 paper that Davy drove the point home in his least compromising manner. Gay-Lussac's reference to acidifying and alkalising principles was ridiculed as 'an attempt to introduce into chemistry a doctrine of occult qualities, and to refer to some mysterious and inexplicable energy what must depend upon a peculiar corpuscular arrangement'.[58] The pitch and the tone of that remark would certainly harmonise with David Knight's thesis that when Davy argued in this way, as he did many times, he was pitting chemistry against the dangers of French materialism.[59] Whether or not this was his deliberate intention, his presuppositions about peculiar corpuscular arrangement would have precluded ascription of acid properties to the presence of hydrogen - an ascription which might have lent itself to reinterpretation in the forbidden format of chemical principles. In short, and ironically, Davy was attacking the very kind of theory a hydrogen theory would have had to be.

Given this extensive list of qualifications, the illuminating question would seem to be not 'How did Davy succeed in anticipating a hydrogen theory of acids?', but rather, 'Why did he fail to do so?'. Divesting that latter question of its whiggish connotations, and insisting on a fully contextual analysis, the answer turns out to be as ironic as

Davy's chemistry was irenic. The ironies I have in mind are enshrined in the following propositions, each of which will be examined in turn:-

1. Although Davy toyed with at least three theories of acidity, he did not actually hold the one later attributed to him.

2. At least two of the three ontologies which at different times he brought to bear on the problem made it impossible for him to hold it.

3. On occasions when Davy was operating with an ontology which might have countenanced a hydrogen theory, it was the very strategy he employed to contest Lavoisier's oxygen theory that diverted him from the contribution of hydrogen.

4. It was Davy's eventual recognition that hydrogen might in some cases contribute to acidity which was in part responsible for his switch to one of the two ontologies which disqualified further generalisation.

5. Until 1812, the year of his <u>Elements of Chemical Philosophy</u>, the recognition of hydrogen as a principle of acidity had arguably been pre-empted by Davy's wishing to keep alive the phlogistic option of hydrogen as the principle of metallicity.

6. Davy's contemporaries and immediate successors who wrongly credited him with a theory which is usually supposed to be right, did so only to show that it was wrong.

7. Davy's pioneer studies in electrochemistry, as

incorporated into the dualistic chemistry of Berzelius, actually inhibited the further understanding of acids.

'Ironic' may seem too strong a label for these propositions as they stand, but each one conceals further ironies which should become clear as we proceed:

1. I have already stressed that Davy did not hold the general theory of acidity to which he has been said to have contributed. His remarks about hydrogen are usually made in a critical context where his immediate objectives are distant from, even contrary to, the construction of a general theory of acids. The point can be registered more forcibly with reference to his paper on the combinations of phosphorus which he read before the Royal Society in April 1818. Even Gregory had to acknowledge that the content of this paper is an embarrassment to the view that Davy's work culminated in a hydrogen theory of acids which then stuck.[60] What the paper shows is that in discussing the phosphorus acids Davy did not stick to a hydrogen formulation, and what it shows above all is that an opportunity to criticise a Frenchman, especially if he were one of the scientific elite,[61] was liable to take priority over the construction of a coherent theory. The victim on this occasion was not Gay-Lussac but Dulong whose work on the compounds of phosphorus Davy attacked on five or six different fronts.[62] In the course of his

critique, Davy presupposes that phosphoric acid contains nothing but phosphorus and oxygen.[63] He notes that Dulong has advanced the 'ingenious opinion, that the hydrophosphorous acid <u>may be considered</u> as a triple compound of hydrogen, oxygen and phosphorus,'[64] but rather than admit a possible similarity between Dulong's view and his own concerning chloric acid, he chooses to press an alternative formulation. On Davy's alternative view, the hydrophosphorous acid is not a triple compound but a compound of phosphoric acid and 'perphosphuretted hydrogen'.[65] Similarly he considers it almost certain that phosphorous acid is a direct combination of phosphorus and oxygen and concludes that the same may be true of the hypophosphorous.[66] What is sustained is not a unified theory of acidity but an assault on Dulong's method of analysis, his combining weights, his confusing compounds with mixtures and even his truthfulness: 'M. Dulong states that no phosphorous acid is formed when phosphorus is burnt in excess of oxygen or atmospheric air; as, he says, I have asserted. I cannot find that I have anywhere made such an assertion: but notwithstanding what M. Dulong pretends, the assertion is true...'.[67] However much Davy's priority disputes[68] and patriotism sensitised his critical apparatus, one cannot escape the conclusion that chemistry was delightful precisely because, like a game of chess, it offered amusement for the mind.[69] It offered opportunities for rigorous argument[70] allied with new experimental moves: the object of the game was not to theorise but to win.

The concealed irony here is that during the course of the nineteenth century the names of Davy and Dulong were frequently associated because they had ostensibly agreed on a hydrogen formulation for acids. In a suggestion which caught the eye of both Gay-Lussac and Ampère,[71] Dulong had envisaged oxalic acid not as a hydrated oxide of carbon but as a compound of hydrogen with carbonic acid. It was an attractive suggestion to contemporaries because it explained the ease with which carbonic acid (CO^2) could be released from oxalates and it has been attractive to historians because it could lead to the conclusion that in salt formation the hydrogen of the acid was directly replaced by a metal.[72] That their names were to be associated by posterity[73] would, I think, have come as a considerable surprise to the antagonists themselves. On at least one occasion Davy deleted Dulong from his manuscript,[74] while, to Berzelius, Dulong wrote in October 1820: 'We have had the honour to be graced for a few days by His Excellency Monseigneur le Chevalier Davy and his chaste wife. He has scarcely deigned to look at me and said but a few words.... You doubtless know that he is going to be nominated President of the Royal Society. It will then be impossible to approach him without prostrating oneself'.[75]

2. Our second irony is that Davy not only did not

hold a hydrogen theory of acids, but that two of the ontologies which he brought to bear on the subject made it impossible for him to do so. If chemical properties depended on corpuscular arrangement or on peculiar combination then, as he wrote in his 1816 paper, 'we have no right to attribute these properties to any of ⟨a compound's⟩ elements to the exclusion of the rest'.[76] Though there are cases where different ontologies appear to co-exist in Davy's Works,[77] more often than not he prefers to play off one against another. There was no reason in theory why an explanation in terms of principles should not be integrated with the other ontologies by postulating that the effect of a 'principle' in any compound would be modified both by the nature of the elements with which it is combined and by their physical arrangement. This was, after all, the way in which the problem was eventually solved. But whether Davy even attempted the integration is far from clear. Two factors at least might have deterred him: his thorough eclecticism and his realisation that there was polemical value in keeping the ontologies distinct.

On the conventional view, Davy came up with a correct theory of acidity in opposition to that of the French chemists. The concealed irony here is not simply that Gay-Lussac entertained in turn the same three approaches as Davy,[78] but that he actually expressed himself, sometimes at least, in a way more conducive to an integration than Davy himself. In his observations on the compounds formed by iodine and chlorine, published in the same year, 1816, as Davy's polemic, Gay-Lussac did not go for mutually exclusive categories. Acidic character, he wrote, 'depends <u>as</u> much on the arrangement <u>as</u> on the energy of the elementary molecules'.[79]

3. The starting point for my third irony is the cyn-ical reconstruction of Davy's outlook offered by J.B. Dumas in his <u>Leçons de la philosophie chimique</u>. According to Dumas, Davy had been so obsessive in his desire to refute every proposition of Lavoisier that since Lavoisier had declared all acids to contain oxygen, out of sheer perversity Davy declared them all to contain hydrogen![80] On the contrary, and herein consists the irony, it was precisely Davy's desire to refute the oxygen theory which prevented a hydrogen theory from taking shape. The reason is simply that the strategy required to depose oxygen was such that when Davy considered acids such as hydrogen chloride and hydrogen iodide, where he might have latched on to the importance of hydrogen, he was so intent on making iodine and chlorine acidifying principles analogous to oxygen that his attention was diverted from the hydrogen. This is certainly true of his celebrated paper on the 'oxymuriatic acid', or chlorine, read before the Royal Society in July 1810. Here, his desire to put chlorine in the same class as oxygen led to his well-known

query: 'may it not in fact be a peculiar acidifying principle, forming compounds with combustible bodies analogous to acids containing oxygen...'[81] It was, however, the further inference that deserves attention. 'On this idea', Davy wrote, 'muriatic acid may be considered as having hydrogen for its basis, and oxymuriatic acid for its acidifying principle'.[82] In other words, the desire to relativise the uniqueness of oxygen by parading additional acidifiers had the effect of keeping hydrogen out of the parade. It had to be a receptor not a donor. This was not a single, isolated inference. It was to the same union with hydrogen that Davy returned when he discussed the combinations of oxymuriatic gas and oxygen. 'Oxymuriatic gas, like oxygen', he explained, 'must be combined in large quantity with peculiar inflammable matter, to form acid matter. In its union with hydrogen, it instantly reddens the driest litmus paper...'[83]

As June Fullmer has recently observed, the strength and direction of Davy's strategy have not always been fully appreciated.[84] Indeed the excitement with which he·proclaimed both fluorine and iodine to be new <u>acidifiers</u> is best seen in his private correspondence. Not even the ape's hoof, he reported, could contain fluorine,[85] which contributed to three particularly powerful acids : hydro-fluoric, silicated fluoric and fluoboric. And when he had concluded his first astonishing study of iodine he could write home to say that as a fourth supporter of combustion it was as useful an ally as he could have found in England.[86] The concealed irony, as Professor Fullmer has so nicely put it, is that the very iodine which Davy so brilliantly characterised had been presented to him with the label 'made in France'.[87] The critical point is that if fluorine, chlorine and iodine were to be genuine allies then they, and not the hydrogen with which they could be combined, had to be the acidifiers. If Davy had any doubts about his strategy they would probably have been quelled by his realisation that chlorine and iodine together produced a compound which was strongly acidic in solution.[88] Even a compound of tin and iodine proved to be acidic : it united with alkalies, so Davy reported to Cuvier, without undergoing decomposition.[89] The irony is, I think, inescapable. As late as the Autumn of 1813 it was Davy's very preoccupation with acidifiers that forced him to turn his back on hydrogen.

4. If hydrogen was disqualified from being an acidifier at a time when Davy's vocabulary still allowed 'principles', our fourth irony concerns the sequel in which an almost converse situation arose. By the time Davy did insist on some contribution from hydrogen, his ontological preconceptions had changed. More to the point, it was his very recognition that hydrogen might contribute which accompanied, perhaps even operated, the ontological switch. Having already

committed himself to the view that the halogens were acidifiers any thought that hydrogen might make a positive contribution was bound to engage him in dialogue with his former self - the only possible out-come being a more emphatic renunciation of 'principles' and a more open adoption of the unitary ontologies which we have seen in the 1816 paper. In other words the recognition that hydrogen was in part responsible had the effect of excluding the grounds on which a more essential contribution might have been generalised.

Two examples from papers published in 1815 should suffice to show that this reconstruction does not violate the textual data. The chemical argument in favour of some role for hydrogen came from a consideration of the acid properties which resulted when the anhydrous solid obtained from iodine and oxygen was dissolved in water. Davy was anxious to apply the word acid to the solution and not to the solid.[90] This meant that the true acid was a 'triple combination of iodine, hydrogen and oxygen'. Since it was well-known that hydrogen combined with iodine produced a very strong acid, Davy's argument took the form of a straight subtraction. If one imagined all the oxygen removed from the iodic acid, from the triple compound, one would still be left with the strong acid hydrogen iodide. For Davy it was therefore a 'fair supposition' that all its elements, and not merely oxygen, must have an influence in producing the acidity of a substance.[91] There is clear evidence here of interdependence between the recognition of a role for hydrogen and the rejection of a 'principle' ontology. The same interdependence is evident too in his subsequent paper on the action of acids on the chlorates.[92] When it had been his object to proclaim the halogens as acidifiers he had referred to hydrogen being acidified by chlorine or iodine. Now, in 1815, following the ontological switch, it is chlorine which 'is capable of being converted into an acid by hydrogen'.[93] For consistency there was only one possible conclusion and Davy immediately drew it : 'Acidity does not depend upon any <u>peculiar</u> elementary substance, but upon <u>peculiar combinations</u> of various substances'.[94] Ironically, hydrogen had contributed to its own downfall.

5. Our fifth irony concerns another sense in which hydrogen had dispossessed itself - in the earlier period when Davy had not yet concluded that a chemistry based on principles was bankrupt. Between 1807 and 1812 when it was at least possible for him to consider hydrogen as a principle of acidity, hydrogen was already spoken for as a principle of metallicity. Davy's attempts to keep alive a modified phlogiston theory have been documented by Siegfried[95] and emphasised by others.[96] To 'inquire whether the metals be capable of being decomposed', was for Davy 'a grand object of true philosophy'.[97] On the hypothesis to which he returned many times their common

ingredient would be hydrogene, the 'cause of metallization'.[98] Hydrogen was therefore associated in Davy's mind with the metallic and the inflammable rather than the acidic.[99]

Davy's motivation for placing hydrogen in the metals is acknowledged to be his well-known desire to minimise the number of genuine chemical elements. If the simplicity and economy of nature demanded a mere handful of elements then hydrogen was the best candidate for one of them.[100] There may even be another sense here in which a hydrogen theory of acids had been pre-empted. One could hardly single out hydrogen as a characteristic component of acids if it was an essential component of almost everything else. 'Our list of simple substances', Davy affirmed, 'will include oxygene, hydrogene, and unknown bases only; metals and inflammable solids will be compounds of these bases with hydrogene... the common acids will be compounds of the same bases with water'.[101] The ulterior irony here is one that all Davy commentators have seen. The more he wished to reduce the number of elements the more he was fated to discover.' It surely was this predicament which made him so slow to abandon altogether an ontology based on principles.[102] The more elements he discovered the greater was his desire to find resemblances between them which could then be attributed to some 'common principle'.[103]

6. Our sixth irony takes us away at last from Davy himself. If he had not insisted on a general correlation between hydrogen and acidity, it is interesting to enquire how it came to be thought that he had. My own reading of the situation is that it was Davy's critics, and Gay-Lussac in particular, who actually invented a general theory which they could fasten on Davy and then explode. The textual support for this interpretation comes from Gay-Lussac's essay on the compounds of iodine and chlorine which he published in February 1816 in the new series of <u>Annales de chimie.</u>[104] Here Gay-Lussac not only quoted a substantial passage from Davy's account of iodic acid,[105] thereby making it available to a succession of French commentators, but also set the trend for associating the names of Davy and Dulong.[106] But the most engaging feature is the subtlety of language by which he teases out of Davy's remarks a generalisation which he can then refute. In the context of his unitary ontology Davy had, as we have seen, referred to chlorine acidified by hydrogen. With a critical aloofness characteristic of Davy himself, Gay-Lussac stopped to say that 'I shall not stop to discuss whether in the hydracids it is the hydrogen which does the acidifying or which is acidified...'[107] But since his object <u>is</u> to comment on Davy's appeal to hydrogen he goes on to say that for the sake of argument he will suppose that hydrogen is the acidifying principle.[108] With this verbal trick he has already extrapolated Davy's

assertion and at the same time reintroduced the vocabulary of principles which Davy had renounced. In subsequent discussion the extrapolation continues. The technique is equally subtle : 'If M. Davy admits that chloric acid owes its acidic properties to hydrogen, why', Gay-Lussac enquired, 'does he not admit that the same is true for sulphuric acid and nitric?'.[109] It is ironic again that Gay-Lussac should alight on two examples which Davy would have accepted![110] Yet there is no denying the fact that it is Gay-Lussac who is trying to force upon Davy the general view which is usually taken to be correct, but with the express purpose of proving it incorrect. Readers of Gay-Lussac's paper would therefore gain the impression that Davy had gone far further than he had in proposing a general theory of acidity. The irony here runs deep because the very argument Gay-Lussac deployed against his caricature of Davy's position was identical to that employed by Davy in reciprocation. The reason the French chemist gave for avoiding the question whether hydrogen is the acidifier or the acidified was the influence of the proportions and the particular <u>arrangement</u> of the constituents in determining the character of a compound.[111]

Two decades later, Davy's position was still being caricatured and rejected, the caricature by then having taken on another aspect which made rejection even easier. The main preoccupation of chemists in the 1830s became the attempt to infer the inner groupings of elements within a compound from the reactions of the compound itself. This particular programme, epitomised by the radical theories of Liebig and Dumas, is one that I have analysed elsewhere.[112] Briefly, the choice of which elements to put into preformed groups was regulated by the need for a dualistic structure, by the quest for analogies between the organic and inorganic compounds, and by a criterion which had become part of chemical practice if not always explicitly so. This was the criterion which dictated that in the event of rival formulations one would opt for those preformed groups which were known to be capable of existing by themselves. If they had been isolated there was a sense in which they were less hypothetical. An acid such as sulphuric would be written in the form $[SO^3 + H^2O]$ because the two parts, sulphur trioxide and water, were both familiar. The relevance of this to acidity theory should become clear if we examine the reasons Dumas gave for rejecting a hydrogen formulation which he attributed to Davy. In a nutshell, Dumas' objection was that if sulphuric acid were written in the form $[H^2 + SO^4]$ one would be postulating the existence of a 'SO^4' group that was entirely hypothetical.[113] Preoccupied with preformed groups in a way that Davy never was,[114] Dumas unconsciously reconstructed Davy's outlook in a form which was as vulnerable as it was a travesty of the original. In a comparison that Davy would have found both poignant and unjust, Dumas declared that the hydrogen system was as bad as the phlogiston theory in requiring as many imaginary bodies as there were acids.[115] That this was a travesty of Davy's position even gave scope for that eccentric chemist, J.J. Griffin, to get his own back at Dumas for the spanking he had received in the Leçons. Suffering the ignominy of finding his nomenclature ridiculed,[116] and the even greater ignominy of finding an 's' on the end of his name, Griffin retaliated on behalf of Davy and himself:

> Dumas ascribes the binary theory of salts to Davy, into whose mouth he puts a speech, which would doubtless have astonished the Fellows of the Royal Society, unused as they are to theatrical displays.[117]

It must also be said that the two chemists who are usually credited with having made a hydrogen theory of acids possible, namely Liebig and Gerhardt, were quite capable, in their more sceptical moments, of urging the same misguided criticism of Davy as that pronounced by Dumas.[118]

7. There is yet one more irony: if it makes sense to say that there were obstacles to the formulation of a hydrogen theory, then Davy contributed to them with the electrochemical researches for which he is most renowned. Although he himself avoided the systematic dualism which came to dominate the

chemistry of the 1820s and '30s, there is no doubt that the theoretical superstructure that Berzelius erected on Davy's pioneering work[119] was largely responsible for the resilience of the /anhydride plus water/ model for the countless acids containing oxygen. Even Davy's own attitude to the respective properties of oxygen and hydrogen was deeply affected by the appearance of oxygen and hydrogen at opposite poles in the electrolysis of water. This is seen most clearly in his notebooks where the twin ideas that hydrogen might be water combined with positive electricity, and oxygen a combination of water and negative electricity, are prominent.[120] The important point is that an antithesis developed in Davy's mind between one series of compounds based on oxygen and another based on hydrogen.[121] In his comments on electrolysis he would make a point of observing that acids and oxygen circulated to one pole whereas alkalies and hydrogen were associated with the other.[122] It was an observation that lay at the very heart of his 'new phlogistic theory'. As he explained in a notebook entry in 1808:

> Oxygene is a principle possessing negative electricity and hydrogene positive. As all the bodies assembling at the pos. contain oxygene so may all the bodies assembling at the neg. contain hyd : and the electricities of ox and hy neutralize each other when they are to each other

as 85 to 15 in weight.[123]
Given his association of acids with the oxygen series it is possible that an antithesis stamped on his mind by the electrolytic process would, certainly until 1812, preclude the association of acids with hydrogen.[124] The antithesis is certainly still there in his <u>Elements of chemical philosophy</u> where he notes that 'of all gaseous substances, hydrogen is most distinctly characterized as an element; and in its relations it is opposed to oxygene'.[125]

It was however the dualism of Berzelius[126] which, endorsed by the electrical dissociation of salts into acids and bases, constituted the more systematic account of chemical combination and at the same time generated a vocabulary for the discussion of acids which undermined any attempt to transpose oxacids into hydracids. In the year following the publication of Davy's <u>Elements</u>, Berzelius published an article in Thomson's <u>Annals of philosophy</u> which, while fighting a rearguard action over the nature of muriatic acid, nevertheless delineated the language that was to be applied to the oxacids. In sulphuric, nitric, oxalic acids, the water, Berzelius declared, 'constitutes a base for the acid'.[127] In other words, even an acid had to comply with an electrochemical dualism by containing within itself an acid and a base. Since the acid anhydrides, to which the term acid was applied in this ulterior sense, frequently contained no hydrogen whatever, it was quite impossible to correlate hydrogen with acidity. The very attempt to give coherence to Davy's electrochemical insights resulted in a rubric which made a general hydrogen theory almost inconceivable.[128] One striking example should clinch the point. Gay-Lussac was reported as having <u>demonstrated</u> that oxalic acid was devoid of hydrogen.[129] The argument was that in the decomposition of oxalic acid by sulphuric, the sulphuric acid was not itself decomposed. If there had been any hydrogen in the oxalic at least some sulphurous acid would be detected. Knowing the great affinity of sulphuric acid for water, it was possible to conclude that the sulphuric had simply removed the water from the hydrated acid. That oxalic acid contained two atoms of carbon and three of oxygen was considered 'incontestable'.[130] If we are tempted to underestimate the power of the /anhydride plus water model/ it is well to remember that Thomas Graham was able to rationalise the different basicities of the phosphorus acids in terms of the amount of combined water they contained.[131] In fact, Dumas saw in the changed basicity of phosphoric acid, following dehydration by heat, a corroboration of the oxacid model, in contrast to which a hydrogen formulation looked distinctly clumsy.[132] The dualistic ontologies derived from electrochemical considerations certainly appear to have made the recognition of displaceable hydrogen more difficult.

That this was true for another reason will perhaps become clear if one recalls that among the many reasons for the submergence of Avogadro's hypothesis during the first half of the nineteenth century was the fact that it could not be reconciled with the electrochemical dualism of Berzelius. It is well known that Avogadro's hypothesis required the postulation of molecules in which an element was in combination with itself - a state of affairs which was literally repulsive on the electrochemical models which became most fashionable. The relevance of this to acidity theory is not remote because, in the absence of incontrovertible methods for atomic and molecular weight determination, the [anhydride plus water] model flourished among monobasic organic acids which, once various corollaries of Avogadro's hypothesis came into force, were deprived of the formulae to which they had become accustomed.[133] As Gerhardt was to insist with unpleasant vehemence, one could not divide the formula of acetic acid by two, still write it in the form of anhydride plus water and retain the strict analogy with sulphuric.[134] It was Gerhardt who, in a work of 1848, volunteered a new definition of acids when he described them as 'salts the base of which is entirely formed by hydrogen .. the hydrogen being exchangable with other metals by double decomposition'.[135] Even here there was to be one last concealed irony. Proponents of the anhydride plus water model would have been delighted had they succeeded in obtaining the anhydride of a monobasic, organic acid. For both Laurent and Gerhardt the dehydration of a single molecule of such an acid was theoretically impossible. Who should be the first to obtain the anhydride but Gerhardt - who, until such time as he could demonstrate beyond doubt that the condensation of two acid molecules had occurred, had played straight into the hand of his opponents.[136]

Using a now famous metaphor, Francis Bacon once described his experimental method as the putting of nature on the rack. Of all the sciences chemistry, by the early nineteenth century, had become the best equipped with instruments of torture. And of all the chemists of the early nineteenth century, there was none more resourceful than Davy in giving nature a good roasting or in applying the new torture of electrocution. Echoing Bacon, Davy himself wrote that experiment 'is as it were the chain that binds down the Proteus of nature, and obliges it to confess its real form and divine origin'.[137] If the study of acidity theory suggests anything it is that nature sometimes has an uncanny way of hitting back. Some of the ironies we have been exposing can almost be traced in the fabric of nature herself[138] who, far from confessing the 'real form' of acidity, remained almost perversely reticent. Although Gerhardt was to redefine acids as compounds containing hydrogen that could be displaced by a metal, there is evidence that he was unhappy with the definition. There were, he said, certain organic substances such as sugars and salicine which contained displaceable hydrogen and yet were palpably not acids.[139] Moreover, and this is a point which has not always been emphasised, to define acidity is not necessarily to explain it. Gerhardt chose to <u>avoid</u> the ontological questions concerning the origin of acidic properties. Even Laurent, who did not,[140] and who would accept a hydrogen definition, persisted in ascribing acid properties to the presence of <u>oxygen</u> spatially exterior to a hydrocarbon prism.[141] The recalcitrance of nature, rather than the economy in which Davy so strongly believed, is one's lasting impression - symbolised perhaps by Gerhardt's repudiation of a hydrogen theory when he eventually composed the fourth volume of his <u>Traité</u>.

In two respects, however, I think Davy would have been pleased by the subsequent turn of events. He, rather than Gay-Lussac, was vindicated on the question whether it was appropriate to use the word acid indiscriminately to refer both to acid anhydrides and to the hydrated species. Davy's discrimination in the case of chloric and iodic acids eventually prevailed on a large scale. Secondly, the use of a hydrogen theory to eliminate the distinction between oxacids and hydracids was sometimes discussed in a manner which indicated that the spirit of Humphry Davy was still abroad. In his elementary textbook of 1855, William Gregory juxtaposed two simple equations for the action of zinc on hydrochloric and sulphuric acids.[143] With the distinction between oxacids and hydracids removed, the two equations had to be strictly parallel:

$$Zn + HSO^4 = ZnSO^4 + H$$
$$Zn + HCl = ZnCl + H$$

The analogy between the two cases would be stronger, Gregory argued, if the chlorine were a complex group like SO^4. His punch line might have been written by Davy: 'it must be remembered that chlorine is only called simple or elementary because we cannot prove it to be compound, not because we know absolutely that it is simple...'.[144]

NOTES

1. A.L. Lavoisier, 'Mémoire sur l'Existence de l'Air dans l'Acide nitreux, et sur les moyens de décomposer & de recomposer cet acide', 1776/1777, cited by H.E. Le Grand, 'Lavoisier's oxygen theory of acidity', <u>Annals of Science</u>, 29 (1972), 1-18, 4.
2. H. Hartley, <u>Humphry Davy</u>, London, 1966, p.105.

3. J.C. Gregory, The scientific achievements of Sir Humphry Davy, Oxford, 1930, p.101.
4. H. Davy, 'The Bakerian Lecture, on some new phenomena of chemical changes produced by electricity, particularly the decomposition of the fixed alkalies...', read Nov. 17, 1807, and published in the Philosophical Transactions of the Royal Society for 1808. See Works, vol.5, pp.57-101, 98. Davy did, in fact, seriously consider that oxygen might exist and form an element in all the true alkalies. R.I. Davy Ms, lecture 10, 1808, Box 2D. By June 1809, Berzelius could write to Davy to say that he had verified a new generalisation : The more oxygen a base contained, the greater the quantity of acid it would neutralise. H.G. Soderbaum (ed.), Jac. Berzelius Bref, Uppsala, 1912-14, vol.1, section 2, p.13. Se also pp.20 and 27.
5. On this point see R. Siegfried, 'Sir Humphry Davy on the nature of the diamond', Isis, 57 (1966), 325-335; and J. Fullmer, 'Davy's priority in the iodine dispute : further documentary evidence', Ambix, 22 (1975), 39-51.
6. Davy to Berzelius, 4 Aug. 1813, in Soderbaum, op.cit. (4), vol.1, section 2, pp.59-60.
7. H.E. Le Grand, 'Berthollet's Essai de statique chimique and acidity', Isis, 67 (1976), 229-238, 232.

8. Ibid., 235. See also D.M. Knight, *The Transcendental Part of Chemistry*, Folkestone, 1978, p.135; and M.P. Crosland, *Gay-Lussac : Scientist and Bourgeois*, Cambridge, 1978, pp.47-9.
9. *Works*, vol.8, p.343.
10. Ibid., vol.5, pp.502 and 507.
11. Ibid., p.507.
12. J.L. Gay-Lussac, 'Observations sur les combinaisons formées par l'iode et par le chlore', *Annales de chimie*, 1 (1816), 157-173, 159.
13. See especially R. Siegfried, 'The mind of Humphry Davy', *Proceedings of the Royal Institution*, 43 (1970), 1-21, 9-11.
14. A typical notebook entry occurs, for example, towards the end of a draft lecture on oxygen for 1809. Under the heading 'Boracic acid', Davy writes : 'Lavoisier's theory will not apply here'. R.I. Davy Ms, Box 3, lecture 3.
15. R.I. Davy Ms, Notebook 20a, p.61. See also R.L. Ziemacki, 'Humphry Davy and the conflict of traditions in early 19th-century chemistry', University of Cambridge PhD dissertation, 1975, p.191.
16. M.P. Crosland, 'Lavoisier's theory of acidity'. *Isis*, 64 (1973), 306-325.
17. Le Grand, loc.cit. (1), 10-12. The most that can be said is that, for Lavoisier, sufficient oxygen was a sufficient condition!
18. Crosland, loc.cit. (16), 320.

19. C.F. Gerhardt, <u>Traité de chimie organique</u>, 4 vols., Paris, 1853-56, vol.4, p.811.
20. C.E. Perrin, 'Lavoisier's table of the elements : a reappraisal', <u>Ambix</u>, 20 (1973), 95-105, 102.
21. H. Le Grand, 'Determination of the composition of the fixed alkalis, 1789-1810', <u>Isis</u>, 65 (1974), 59-65, 63.
22. <u>Works</u>, vol.5, p.100. One commentator has even gone so far as to say that, at this stage, Davy 'seems to have had an even higher regard for oxygen than Lavoisier himself ..', P. Collins, 'Humphry Davy and heterogeneous catalysis', <u>Ambix</u>, 22 (1975), 205-217, 206.
23. Davy to Berzelius, 18 Oct. 1809, in Soderbaum, op.cit. (4), vol.1, section 2, p.16. In supporting this conjecture, Davy was actually presupposing an oxygen theory of acids, for he was impressed with the acidic nature of tellurium hydride. Since it was unlikely that the metal contained the oxygen, one could postulate it in the hydrogen. Knight, op.cit. (8), p.133.
24. Berzelius to Davy, Aug./Sept. 1812, in Soderbaum, ibid., 31-35, 33.
25. R. Siegfried, 'The discovery of potassium and sodium, and the problem of the chemical elements', <u>Isis</u>, 54 (1963), 247-258, especially 255-57. See also the joint paper by Siegfried and B.J. Dobbs, 'Composition, a neglected aspect of the chemical revolution', <u>Annals of Science</u>, 24 (1968), 275-293, 288.

26. Davy to Berzelius, 4 Aug. 1813, in Soderbaum, op.cit. (4). vol.1, section 2, p.59.
27. Berzelius, 'On the nature of muriatic acid', Annals of Philosophy, 2 (1813), 255; 'A comparison of the old and new theories respecting the nature of oxymuriatic acid', ibid., 7 (1816), 273.
28. M. Crosland, 'Theories of acidity in the early nineteenth century', Proceedings of the XIIIth International Congress of the History of Science, Moscow, (1971), 67-74.
29. On this point see also Siegfried, loc.cit. (5). 327.
30. Gregory, op.cit. (3), p.103.
31. Ibid., p.102. The emphasis is Gregory's.
32. Davy, 'On the analogies between the undecompounded substances, and on the constitution of acids', Quarterly Journal of Science, 1 (1816), 283-288, 287.
33. Ibid., 287.
34. On this essential point I am in complete agreement with Knight, op.cit. (8), pp.137-8.
35. In his first geology lecture of 1811, Davy wrote: 'So different are the exertions of the faculties of the mind, and so infinitely various the combinations of our ideas; that the same ovjects may be examined with the most opposite views ..'. And from the 4th geology lecture of 1805: 'It has often happened during the progress of science that two doctrines immediately

opposite have been supported with great powers of reasoning and almost with equal plausibility .. '. R.I. Davy Ms, notebook 16d.

36. *Works*, vol.8, p.312. For a further discussion of this epistemological issue see R. Siegfried, 'The chemical philosophy of Humphry Davy', *Chymia*, 5 (1959), 193-201, especially 194 and 198-9.
37. *Fragmentary remains*, p.54.
38. *Works*, vol.5, p.138.
39. Knight, op.cit. (8), p.148.
40. On the particular form of Davy's eclecticism see C.A. Russell, 'The electrochemical theory of Sir Humphry Davy. Part 3. The evidence of the Royal Institution manuscripts', *Annals of Science*, 19 (1963), 255-271, especially 270; and Crosland, op.cit. (8), pp.88 and 89.
41. Davy, loc.cit. (32).
42. Ibid., 285.
43. Gay-Lussac and Thenard, 'Observations sur trois mémoires de Mr. Davy..'. *Bibliotheque britannique, ou recueil extrait des ouvrages anglais périodiques..*, 45 (1810), 133-160, especially 134-6.
44. If water were excluded from the formulation of sulphuric acid $[SO_3 + H_2O]$, then the SO_3 remaining could never be envisaged as a hydracid since it contained no hydrogen.

45. From the conclusion to the manuscript version of Davy's paper entitled 'Some experiments on a solid compound of iodine and oxygene, and on its chemical agencies', published in <u>Phil. Trans.</u>, 105 (1815), 203-213, and in <u>Works</u>, vol.5, concluding on p.502. The manuscript version is to be found between pp.282 and 283 of Faraday's copy of J.A. Paris, <u>Life</u>. Faraday's copy is held by the Royal Institution.
46. Gay-Lussac's stance on this particular issue was firmly expressed: 'Si je ne me suis point fait illusion, il n'est pas nécessaire d'avoir deux noms pour désigner, comme l'a fait M. Davy, l'acide iodique sans eau et l'acide iodique combiné avec elle. La dénomination <u>acide iodique</u> peut s'appliquer indistinctement à ces deux états, puisque l'eau ne change point les propriétés acides ..'. Gay-Lussac, loc.cit. (12), 170.
47. Davy, loc.cit. (32), 288.
48. Davy, manuscript draft of ibid., R.I. Davy Ms, Box 10, 24-46, 41.
49. Davy, Commonplace Book, R.I. Davy Ms, 176.
50. For a further example, involving the role of water in the chlorine controversy, see Knight, op.cit. (8), pp.136-7.
51. Ampère, 'D'une classification naturelle pour les corps simples', <u>Annales de chimie</u>, 1 (1816), 295, 296 and 301. On Davy's debt to Ampère, see K.R. and D.L. Gardiner, 'Ampère and his

English acquaintances', <u>British Journal for the History of Science</u>, 2 (1964-5), 235-45, 236-7.
52. Davy, loc.cit. (32), 283.
53. Ibid., 283.
54. Davy, <u>Elements of Chemical Philosophy</u>, London, 1812, p.490.
55. Davy, loc.cit. (32), 283-4.
56. Ibid., 284.
57. Ibid., 285.
58. Ibid., 285.
59. Knight, op.cit. (8), pp.61-90.
60. Gregory, op.cit. (3), p.103.
61. As Crosland has observed (op.cit. (8), p.83), Davy may be regarded as a natural <u>ally</u> of the French chemists who found themselves outside the French scientific establishment. Whether Davy's own perception of his relations with the two groups would reflect the same contrast between insiders and outsiders would seem to be another question.
62. Davy, 'New experiments on some of the combinations of phosphorus', <u>Phil. Trans.</u>, 108 (1818), 316-337; <u>Works</u>, vol.5, pp.369-390.
63. Ibid., <u>Works</u>, vol.5, p.381.
64. Ibid., p.385. The emphasis is Davy's.
65. Ibid., pp.385-89.
66. Ibid., pp.389-90.
67. Ibid., p.389.

68. On the iodine priority new documentary evidence has recently been brought to light by Fullmer loc.cit. (5), and by Crosland op.cit. (8), pp.84-85 and 269-70, both of which reveal how intense the rivalry was. The claims and counter-claims were complicated by the fact that Gay-Lussac not only wanted the recognition that he felt was rightly his but also suspected that for the interpretation of chlorine and fluorine Davy was more indebted to Ampère than he cared to acknowledge. This was a charge that Davy rebutted (see loc.cit. (32), pp.284-85). Yet it has to be said that the manuscript draft of that rebuttal reveals a Davy in a state of some indecision as to how he might best present his case - particularly on the interpretation of fluorine where he had first resisted and then resumed Ampère's line; R.I. Davy Ms, Box 10, 24-46, especially the several alterations in the draft of the footnote.
69. Davy himself wrote of his chemical hypotheses that they should be 'the instruments of thought, - the secret amusements of the mind..' Works, vol.1, pp.152-53.
70. It was, in fact, one of Davy's chief complaints that in chemical philosophy there was the 'necessity of more rigid reasoning'. Fragmentary remains, p.202.
71. Ampère, loc.cit. (51), 298.

72. P. Lemay and R.E. Oesper, 'Pierre Louis Dulong - his life and work', *Chymia*, 1 (1948), 171-190, 174.
73. Dumas, in particular, was to stress that to Davy's theory 'M. Dulong a prêtè son appui si puissant à nos yeux', *Leçons de la philosophie chimique*, Paris, 1837, p.337. See also p.340. The same association was affirmed by Gerhardt, op.cit. (19), vol.4, pp.812-3.
74. Davy, manuscript draft of note 32, R.I. Davy Ms, Box 10, 36-7.
75. Dulong to Berzelius, 2 Oct. 1820, in Soderbaum, op.cit. (4), vol.2, section 1, pp.17-18.
76. Davy loc.cit. (32), 286.
77. In his 1816 paper (see note 32), for example, Davy writes as if an explanation in terms of 'peculiar combination' is the same as an explanation in terms of corpuscular arrangement. Earlier, as in his *Elements of Chemical Philosophy*, he would align chlorine with oxygen as an elementary supporter of combustion, yet at the same time insist that the process of combustion did not require peculiar substances; Siegfried, loc.cit. (5), 331. In his paper on iodine despatched from Paris in December 1813, his line of thought follows the resemblances between chlorine, oxygen and iodine as acidifying principles, yet it stops with the conclusion that acidity 'seems to depend upon peculiar combinations of matter,

and not on any peculiar principle'. <u>Works</u>, vol.5, p.456. It is not even clear whether he meant 'on any <u>one</u> peculiar principle' or 'on principles in general'.
78. Crosland, loc.cit. (28), 72.
79. Gay-Lussac, loc.cit. (12), 157. I do not, however, wish to imply that Gay-Lussac was consistently this subtle. For a more detailed evaluation see Crosland, op.cit. (8), pp.131-34.
80. Dumas, op.cit. (73), p.337.
81. Davy, 'Researches on the oxymuriatic acid, its nature and combinations ...', <u>Phil. Trans.</u>, 100 (1810), 231-257; <u>Works</u>, vol.5, pp.284-311, 297.
82. Ibid., <u>Works</u>, vol.5, p.297.
83. Davy, 'The Bakerian Lecture. On some of the combinations of oxymuriatic gas and oxygene ..', <u>Phil. Trans.</u>, 101 (1811), 1-35; <u>Works</u>, vol.5, pp.341-42.
84. Fullmer, loc.cit. (5), 44.
85. <u>Memoirs</u>, vol.1, p.459. Humphry explicitly referred to fluorine as a 'new acidifier', and observed that 'We have now a triad of supporters of combustion'. This letter to John is dated 4 April 1813 and is also reproduced in <u>Fragmentary Remains</u>, pp.178-9.
86. Humphry to John Davy, 18 March 1814, in <u>Fragmentary Remains</u>, pp.186-7.
87. Fullmer, loc.cit. (5), 40.

88. Davy, 'Some experiments and observations on a new substance which becomes a violet-coloured gas by heat', *Phil. Trans.*, 104 (1814), 74-93; *Works*, vol.5, pp.437-456, 441-2.
89. Fullmer, loc.cit. (5), 46. In one of his notebooks Davy also noted that 'Iron with iodine gave a deep red acid solution to water precipitable by ammonia ...', R.I. Davy Ms, Notebook 15c, 43.
90. Davy, loc.cit. (45), *Works*, vol.5, p.502.
91. Ibid., p.502.
92. Davy, 'On the action of acids on the salts usually called hyperoxymuriates, and on the gases produced from them', *Phil. Trans.*, 105 (1815), 214-219; *Works*, vol.5, pp.503-509.
93. Ibid., *Works*, vol.5, p.508.
94. Ibid. The emphasis is Davy's.
95. R. Siegfried, 'The phlogistic conjectures of Humphry Davy', *Chymia*, 9 (1964), 117-124.
96. Especially by Ziemacki, op.cit. (15).
97. *Works*, vol.8, p.331; Siegfried and Dobbs, loc.cit. (25), 290.
98. Davy, 'The Bakerian lecture for 1809. On some new electrochemical researches .... and on some combinations of hydrogen', *Phil. Trans.*, 100 (1810), 16-74, 69. His belief that the metals had in common 'a principle that causes their similitude' was reiterated, together with the analogy between the amalgams of ammonium and the metals which sustained the view that

hydrogen was the principle, in his lecture on the metals delivered on 10 April 1812 and recorded in the Faraday Notebook, R.I. Faraday Ms, 355-6.

99. Hence Davy's enthusiasm for tellurium as a reagent when he first appreciated its strong affinity for hydrogen: 'Should tellurium <u>really</u> posses a strong attraction for hydrogene it will be the most valuable discovery of a reagent perhaps ever made. It will lead to test facts of the phlogistic and antiphlogistic theories'. R.I. Davy Ms, Laboratory Notebook, 1809-1812, August 1809, 14. Hence also his concern 'to try if the metals can be extra hydruretted', R.I. Davy Ms, Notebook 13j, 49.

100. Davy, op.cit. (54), p.481.

101. Davy, loc.cit. (98), 69.

102. Levere, for example, has quite correctly drawn attention to the fact that Davy experienced something of the 'conflict between the demands of design and the achievements of research'. T.H. Levere, 'The rich economy of nature: chemistry in the nineteenth century', in U.C. Knoepflmacher and G.B. Tennyson (eds.), <u>Nature and the Victorian Imagination</u>, Berkeley, 1977, pp.189-200, 196.

103. Davy, loc.cit. (83), <u>Works</u>, vol.5, p.347, footnote: 'It is possible that oxymuriatic gas may be compound, <u>and that this body and oxygen may contain some common principle</u>; but at present

we have no more right to say that oxymuriatic gas contains oxygen than to say that tin contains hydrogen ...'. The emphasis is mine. If one were tempted to develop the point, and if one were prepared to accept that Davy was concerned to go through the motions, at least, of attacking French materialism, then one might be able to say that two of the strategies he employed were not entirely compatible. To affirm the reality of design in nature he wanted to minimise the number of genuine elements. But to achieve <u>that</u> he was obliged to have recourse to the very ontology based on principles which, when used by a Frenchman, had become a symbol of 'materialism' and an object of his derision.

104. Gay-Lussac, loc.cit. (12).
105. Ibid., 159.
106. Ibid., 167.
107. Ibid., 166.
108. Ibid., 166: 'comme j'ai ici pour objet de considérer la propriété qu'a l'hydrogène d'entrer comme partie essentielle dans plusieurs acides, je supposerai que c'est lui qui est le principe acidifiant'.
109. Ibid., 167.
110. As Davy himself reported, 'M. Gay-Lussac states, that if the chloric acid be not admitted as a pure combination of chlorine and oxygene, neither can the nitric or sulphuric acids be admitted as pure combinations of

oxygene. This is perfectly obvious', loc.cit. (32), 287.
111. Gay-Lussac, loc.cit. (12), 166.
112. J.H. Brooke, 'Laurent, Gerhardt and the philosophy of chemistry', Historical Studies in the Physical Sciences, 6 (1975), 405-429.
113. Dumas, op.cit. (73), Lesson 9, p.341.
114. A typical passage which reveals that Davy was not animated by the desire to define a unique solution for each constitutional problem, in terms of preferred preformed groups, occurs in one of his notebooks: 'Water probably essential to nitric acid. Oxygene, hydrogene and nitrogen under different modifications probably form also the ammoniacal and nitrous compounds. Nitrate of ammonia becomes, either nit. acid and ammonia or nitrous acid nitrous gas and azote with water or nitrous oxide and water..'. R.I. Davy Ms, notebook 13j, 116-115.
115. Dumas, op.cit. (73), p.342.
116. Ibid., p.354-5.
117. J.J. Griffin, The Radical Theory in Chemistry, London, 1858, p.20.
118. J. von Liebig, 'Sur la constitution des acides organiques', Annales de chimie, 68 (1838), 72 and 84; Gerhardt, op.cit. (19), vol.4, p.815.
119. For Berzelius' acknowledged debt to Davy, see C.A. Russell, 'The electrochemical theory of Sir Humphry Davy. Part 2: Electrical inter-

pretations of chemistry'. *Annals of Science*, 15 (1959), 15-25, 24.
120. A particularly clear record of these ideas may be found in notebook 13j, R.I. Davy Ms, 44.
121. For a full discussion of this aspect of Davy's outlook, see Ziemacki, op.cit.(15), 255-264.
122. This same dichotomy reappeared in his Bakerian lecture for 1826, 'On the relations of electrical and chemical changes', *Phil. Trans.*, 116 (1826), 383-422, 407; C.A. Russell,'The electrochemical theory of Sir Humphry Davy. Part 1: The voltaic pile and electrolysis', *Annals of Science*, 15 (1959), 1-13, 8.
123. R.I. Davy Ms, notebook 13j, 146-144.
124. Note, for example, Davy's reference the 'hydrogene side of the pile' in notebook 22b, 60.
125. Davy, op.cit. (54), p.254.
126. For an introduction to the electrochemical dualism of Berzelius, see C.A. Russell, 'The electrochemical theory of Berzelius', Parts 1 and 2, *Annals of Science*, 19 (1963), 117-145. On the extension of the dualistic rubric into organic chemistry, see J.H. Brooke, 'Chlorine substitution and the future of organic chemistry: methodological issues in the Laurent - Berzelius correspondence', *Studies in the History and Philosophy of Science*, 4 (1973), 47-94.
127. Berzelius, 'On the nature of muriatic acid', loc.cit. (27), 254.

128. The persistence of this theoretical constraint may be discerned in a text-book of Pelouze and Frémy who, in the late 1840s were still referring to SO^2 as sulphurous acid anhydride, CO^2 as carbonic acid and still cashing in on the fact that the one could directly replace the other from dry sodium carbonate. Cours de chimie générale, Paris, 1848-50, vol.1, p.331.
129. Gay-Lussac, Cours de chimie, 2 vols., Paris, 1828, vol.2, lesson 24, p.5.
130. Ibid., p.2.
131. T. Graham, 'Researches on the arseniates, phosphates, and modifications of phosphoric acid', Phil. Trans., 123 (1833), 253f. Graham could write the tribasic phosphoric acid in the form $PO^5 + 3HO$, the dibasic pyrophosphoric acid $PO^5 + 2HO$, and the monobasic metaphosphoric acid $PO^5 + HO$. The correlation of basicity with the proportion of combined water was obviously attractive and the presence of a common PO^5 group had a similar unifying effect. It allowed Graham to say that 'there is only one phosphoric acid, and that the modifications are entirely due to the quantity of water combined with the acid'. Ibid., 283. See also J.R. Partington, A History of Chemistry, 4 vols., London 1964, vol.4, pp.272-5.
132. Dumas (note 73), pp.342-3. On Dumas' notation, the three phosphoric acids could be written in the elegant form $P^2O^5, 3H^2O \ldots P^2O^5, 2H^2O \ldots$

P^2O^5, H^2O. To capture their respective basicities by a <u>hydrogen</u> theory would, however, require the less unified scheme: P^2O^8, H^6 ... P^2O^7, H^4 ... P^2O^6, H^2. As Dumas himself observed, 'Voilà de bien graves changemens de nature pour des corps qui passent si aisément de l'un à l'autre'. For the significance of Graham's work in relation to Liebig's reconsideration of the oxacid/hydracid distinction, see F. Holmes, 'Liebig', in C.C. Gillispie (ed.), <u>Dictionary of Scientific Biography</u>, New York and London, 1973, vol.8, pp.338-341.

133. I do not wish to imply by this that the acceptance of Avogadro's hypothesis in the second decade of the 19th century would have miraculously solved all the problems associated with the determination of atomic and molecular weights - as has often been suggested. For an account of some of the traps which this subject has set, see J.H. Brooke, 'Avogadro's hypothesis and its fate : a case-study in the failure of case-studies', <u>History of Science</u> (forthcoming). That the organic acids came to have twice the number of atoms than we should now countenance followed from the equivalent adopted for silver in the determination of their silver salts. The problem was diagnosed, albeit controversially, by Gerhardt in his 'Recherches sur la classification chimique', <u>Revue scientifique et industrielle</u>, 12

(1843), 594-600.

134. The conventional analogy was between $SO^3 + H^2O$ and $[C^4H^6]O^3 + H^2O$. To divide the latter by two immediately destroyed it. Accordingly, Gerhardt proclaimed that 'sur les cent et quelques acides organiques aujourd'hui connus à peine s'il y en a quatre ou cinq capables de perdre les éléments de l'eau, de manière à se prêter à la théorie binaire'. Ibid., 595.

135. Gerhardt, <u>Introduction à l'étude de la chimie par le système unitaire</u>, Paris, 1848, pp.103-4.

136. When Gerhardt prepared acetic anhydride from acetyl chloride and sodium acetate (<u>Comptes rendus de l'Académie des sciences</u>, 34 (1852), 755), this did not constitute proof that two acetyl groups were present in each anhydride. Indeed, the fact that Gerhardt had prepared an organic acid anhydride at all was claimed as a victory for his opponents, just as Deville's isolation of nitric anhydride had provided a circular verification of the anhydride plus water model. (L.E. Grimaux and C. Gerhardt, <u>Charles Gerhardt. Sa vie, son oeuvre, sa corréspondance</u>, Paris, 1900, p.234f.) As A.W. Hofmann reported (<u>Medical Times and Gazette</u>, 9 (1854), 563), Gerhardt's anhydride was 'hailed with great delight in the camp of the followers of [the traditional] theory, and regarded by many as the key-stone of the edifice'.

137. Davy, op.cit. (54), p.503.
138. How could Graham, for example, have guessed that the conversion of phosphoric into pyrophosphoric acid involved the dehydration of two acid molecules, thereby vitiating his elegant scheme (cf. notes 131 and 132)?
139. Gerhardt, op.cit. (135), p.108.
140. For the contrast between the presuppositions of Laurent and Gerhardt, see Brooke loc.cit. (112).
141. Proposition 8 of his doctoral thesis included this assertion: 'Lorsque le corps deshydrogénant, l'oxigène par example, entrera dans la combinaison, mais hors du radical, il la rendra acide, quelque grand que soit la quantité de carbone, d'hydrogène, et d'oxigène entrant dans le radical, l'acidité ne dépendant nullement du rapport du carbone et de l'hydrogène à l'oxigène, mais seulement de la place de celui-ci', Annales de chimie, 61 (1836), 128. In his Chemical Method, almost twenty years later, he was still writing the organic acids with a spotlight on their external oxygen; Chemical Method, transl. by W. Odling, London 1855, p.331.
142. Gerhardt, op.cit. (19), vol.4, pp.814-16.
143. W. Gregory, Elementary Treatise on Chemistry, Edinburgh, 1855, p.81.
144. Ibid., p.81.

Davy's 'Intellectual Delight' and his Lectures at the Royal Institution

Robert Siegfried

The theme of this paper is that the psychological origin of Davy's creativity lay in the intrinsic excitement he experienced in the acquisition of rational understanding; as a scientist he sought that understanding in the investigation of nature; as a religious man of his own time he saw divine purpose in the natural order; as a man of high morality he felt the obligation to convey to others his own understanding of that order and purpose. But the experiential basis of this sequence was his own pleasure in the discovery of new truths. His old and intimate friend, Thomas Poole, expressed it clearly when he wrote that Davy's 'delight was in his intellectual being. He felt that he had the power of investigating the laws of nature beyond that entrusted to the generality of men ...'[1]

Everyone familiar with Davy's life will sense the validity of Poole's comment, but this aspect of Davy's character has never been explored. The man who 'bounded about the room in ecstatic delight' when the 'first globules of potassium burst through the crust of potash',[2] could not properly convey that excitement in the disciplined language of the <u>Philosophical Transactions</u> of the Royal Society. But his lectures at the Royal Institution provided a most fitting outlet for the expression of his intellectual delight. The very purpose of those lectures was to persuade his audiences, chiefly members of the privileged classes, to become patrons of science through their support of the Institution itself. The 'intellectual enjoyment' that he offered them as a reward would come in their larger and brighter vision of the order and design in nature by which everything was made subservient to the preservation of life on earth. This message is preached with such frequency and insistence that we can safely attribute its origin to the sense of obligation Davy felt to utilize 'his uncommon powers' not only in the discovery of the laws of nature, but in conveying to the world the resulting sense of wonder and awe that he so clearly felt.

From the very beginning of his association with the Royal Institution, Davy appears to have foreseen his role as public moralist for science. Just prior to his departure from Bristol to take up his new duties in London, he wrote to his first patron, Davies Giddy,

> The Royal Institution will, I hope, be of some utility to society. It has undoubtedly the capability of becoming a great instrument of moral and

> intellectual improvement. Its funds are
> very great. It has attached to it the
> feelings of a great number of people of
> fashion and property, and consequently
> may be the means of employing, to useful
> purposes, money which would otherwise be
> squandered in luxury, and in the
> reproduction of unnecessary labour'.[3]

Whether or not the managers of the Royal Institution saw Davy's role in the same way as did Davy himself, they quickly recognized his success in attracting large audiences drawn from the leisured and fashionable classes, audiences whose annual subscriptions paid the bills of the previous season. By 1804 the Institution had undergone changes in its original purpose to take advantage of Davy's popular success by attempting to give 'fashion to science'.[4] Davy's success in making science fashionable is attested by many contemporary witnesses[5] and his eloquence in this endeavour was particularly noted by Louis Simond touring England from America in 1811.

> His lectures are frequently figurative
> and poetical; and he is occasionally
> carried away ... into the depths of moral
> philosophy and of religion. You foresee
> by a certain tuning or pitching of the
> organ of speech to a graver key,
> thrusting of his chin into his neck,

> and even pulling out his cravat, when
> Mr. Davy is going to be eloquent,- for he
> rarely yields to the inspiration till he
> is duly prepared. I have heard the moral
> digressions ... and his solemn appeals
> to the supreme wisdom severely criticised;
> but the greatest part of his audience
> hears them with delight and applause,
> and I think Mr. Davy would disarm
> criticism, if he abandoned himself more
> naturally to his spontaneous feelings...[6]

The high proportion of women in Davy's audiences, 'principally matrons and their young daughters, who take notes', was noted by many observers.[7] But this was consonant with Davy's purposes, for it was through women that the values he was promoting could be most effectively preserved and extended.

> The standard of the consideration and
> importance of females in society is, I
> believe, likewise the standard of
> civilisation. The leisure of the higher
> classes is so great, their influence
> so strong, that it is almost their duty
> to endeavour to awaken and keep alive
> the love of improvement. It is only
> ignorance or selfishness which can wish
> to prevent the diffusion of knowledge.

> It is the grand privilege of human
> nature; it is the lamp which guides
> our steps amidst the obscurity of things,
> which preserved the mind awake to its
> just interests, carrying it from
> transient and trifling objects to
> those which are permanent and useful;
> affording a noble employment in youth,
> a delightful consolation in age;
> teaching that in all things there is
> order, and harmony, and wisdom;
> exalting the sensual into the
> intellectual, and the intellectual
> into the moral and religious being.[8]

The moral philosophy expressed in Davy's lectures can be analysed into three distinguishable themes, often conjointly presented. It was not until his posthumously published <u>Consolations in Travel</u>, however, that he consciously attempted their philosophical unity, but in both the lectures and the <u>Consolations</u> the aim, the method, and the rewards are the same. Within this position the purpose of human life was the promotion of scientific understanding of nature through the utilization of man's unique rationality. The process for achieving that progress was the reliance on facts and the concommitant distrust of theoretical conjecture as too liable to human error. The reward for the efforts made was the intellectual enjoyment, the mental gratification derived from the ever clearer perception of the wisdom and the providential design in the laws of nature.

Before providing illustrations of these themes it is appropriate to offer a few comments about the corpus of surviving lectures in the archives of the Royal Institution. Davy took no obvious care to preserve the manuscripts of his lectures and we are fortunate that so many as seventy odd of them still exist. Most are written out fully in Davy's own hand on large sheets of paper, and many show corrections, deletions, and additions as if modified for re-use. There is no pattern among them to account for their particular survival, except for the ten geology lectures of 1805 which were written in bound notebooks rather than on loose sheets. Because this series constitutes the only complete course among the survivors, illustrations of Davy's themes are drawn chiefly from this source.[9]

References to providential design occur throughout these lectures and serve as a kind of unifying motif. Early in the first lecture Davy called attention to the order to be discerned in the structure of the earth in spite of the apparent disarray. Although the knowledge of this order is useful to the miner, the engineer, the drainer, and the improver of land, Davy placed greater emphasis on 'the usefulness of the knowledge of nature in increasing mental enjoyment and in strengthening and exalting our sentiments', a subject which, he said, needed no elaboration for it had been 'often discharged in this room'. But geology offered some 'particular intellectual effects' of this sort.

> The study of the constitution of the globe, of the manner in which its changes are produced and of the laws by which dead and inorganic matter are rendered subservient to the purposes of living beings, affords some of the most sublime objects which can ever occupy our contemplation.

From the middle of the first lecture and extending through the fourth, Davy presented a long historical account of geological and cosmological writings, beginning with the Egyptians and Hindoos, through the Greek and Roman writers, up to the contemporary authors James Hutton and A.G. Werner. The remaining six lectures are chiefly descriptive presentation of major topics accompanied by appropriate comments on scientific procedure and illustrations of divine providence. The fifth lecture was devoted to the primitive rocks, those classified today as igneous and metamorphic; lectures six and seven to secondary rocks, roughly equivalent to our sedimentary class. Davy's identification of basalt as a secondary rock reflects one of the unresolved problems of that time, for though like many of his contemporaries he recognised the volcanic source of many basaltic formations, he believed others to be conformable with associated rocks of aqueous origin. Metallic veins were the subject in number eight, while volcanoes were discussed in number nine and the first half of ten. In the last half of the final lecture Davy returned to providential design as a summarizing theme for the entire course.

The devotion of four lectures to the history of geological thought may seem excessive, but if we recognize that in 1805 there was still no clearly defined rational structure for geological knowledge, the historical background may be seen as an effective alternative for the discussion of contemporary geological problems. This approach also gave Davy the opportunity to illustrate how good science should be done, and to show the development of proper scientific procedure. It is in the criticism of early writers that Davy's extreme distrust of theoretical conjectures shows most clearly. For Davy it was facts and facts alone that formed the reliable basis of scientific understanding. Every writer considered is evaluated according to how closely he conformed to this ideal.

Few of the ancient philosophers measured up: 'It appeared to all the philosophers [of the Pythagorean school] more easy to imagine than to observe, and more amusing to dream than to reason'.

Theophrastus 'is the first of the ancients who has any claim to the title of geologist or mineralogist', yet he had no successors 'to trust like him to facts, and to record only the results of experience and accurate observations'. [Lect. 2]

Francis Bacon, in Davy's view, 'was the first philosopher who laid down plans for extending knowledge of universal application, who ventured to assert that all the sciences could be nothing more than expressions of facts and that the first step towards the attainment of real discovery was the humiliating confession of ignorance'. But it was Robert Hooke who first applied a true Baconian attitude to geological matters, by contenting himself with 'demonstrating a certain part of the existing order of nature without attempting a general system of the past changes of the globe and of its future destiny'. [Lect. 3]

This critical attitude toward system builders is no less apparent when he reached the contemporary writers on geology, including Werner and Hutton, the central figures of the Neptunian and Plutonian views of the origin of the earth's crustal rocks. The central criticism offered to Werner's Neptunian theory was simply that the rocky materials are not soluble in water, hence could not have precipitated from a primordial ocean as the theory described. The corresponding criticism of Hutton's theory was that in the absence of any demonstrable evidence that materials such as quartz could be melted by any known heat, it was poor science to argue that it had crystallized from a molten state.

> If Dr. Hutton and Mr. Werner had contented themselves with explaining those operations by which our globe is constantly preserved as a habitable world in the series of events at present taking place, they would have deserved a much higher praise than that of having been the founders of ingenious hypotheses. But when attempting to explain appearances they attribute to agents powers which they have never been observed to exert, or refer effects to causes the operation of which they are ignorant, their suppositions do not merit the name of science. ⎡Lect. 5⎤

Davy's belief in the providential design is illustrated again in the passage above, and was not based on a literal interpretation of the scriptures. The revealed truth of the Scriptures and the truth to be found in nature formed a general harmony, not a detailed correspondence. He was very critical of those writers who appeared to use scriptural accounts to confirm their own hypotheses. Of Thomas Burnet's <u>Sacred Theory of the Earth</u> he said it 'affords one proof amongst many others of the folly of attempts to wrest the meaning of the sacred writings, which express general truths, so as to make them serve as supports for hypotheses of human invention, so as to blend them with the visions and fancies of men'. ⟦Lect. 3⟧ He made similar criticisms of the system of de Luc, Whitehurst, and Kirwan. ⟦Lect. 4⟧ Only the 'celebrated Leibniz' escaped his criticism on this point, for,

> In his <u>Protogaea</u> published in 1693 he enters upon the great doctrines relating to the globe, the primary creation, the deluge, the changes that have been since produced and that will be produced in future ages. He assumes as the foundation of his reasoning the account of the creation given in the sacred writings.
>
> The work ... is worthy of the genius of the illustrious author. When facts are stated in it they are detailed with clearness and accuracy, and where hypotheses are indulged in, they mark an imagination fertile in novelty and pregnant with bold conceptions. ⟦Lect. 3⟧

There are passages in which Davy's faith in providential design is so clear that it seems to question the propriety of even investigating the origins of things. 'Where we can perceive no certain indication of a prior arrangement, there it is reasonable for us to rest, there it is reasonable for us to fix the foundations of our science'. /Lect. 5/ And Davy said that de Luc, in interpreting the Biblical account of the origins in geological terms, had allowed his genius 'to waste its strength in vain attempts to penetrate into mysteries which have been wisely concealed from man ...'. Yet later in the same lecture Davy expressed admiration for the daring of man 'to endeavour to apply his mind to the most recondite operations which have been produced by divine intelligence, to attempt to explain the changes that have taken place beneath the foundations of the earth, to examine the great laws of the creation, of the systems of the universe, and to reason concerning their origin in that infinite space which he is wholly unable to penetrate or even accurately to imagine'. /Lect. 4/ The ambivalence expressed here in 1805 are resolved more positively toward the use of the intellect in a passage from a geology lecture of 1811: 'the laws of Infinite Wisdom cannot be fully estimated by finite intelligence; yet there is a glory in the effort, and delight and instruction in the result'.[11]

In lecture five Davy began the substantive segments of the course with an extensive description of the appearance, distribution, and composition of the primitive rocks. He noted they can be found in the deepest mines and on the highest mountains, and are common in all the continents of the earth. The extended discussion of these crystalline rocks allowed him to make more detailed criticisms of the Wernerian and Huttonian theories of their origins.

Lectures six and seven were principally concerned with secondary rocks, especially those containing fossils. These, Davy said,

> are monuments of the great change that the globe has undergone. They exhibit indubitable evidences of a former order of things and of a great destruction and renovation of living beings ... [The secondary strata were produced by] the great inundation of the waters upon the land recorded both in sacred and profane history ... We perceive the effects of this great catastrophe but the immediate natural cause of it can never be satisfactorily developed.
> [Lects. 6 and 7]

In spite of his assertion that the 'immediate natural cause' of the great inundation can never be satisfactorily developed, Davy none the less gave an entirely speculative elaboration of the scheme of Leibniz as extended by William Whiston. A comet passing near the earth might, by its gravitational attraction, raise the waters of the oceans to vast heights from which they would inundate the globe. As if in apology for this excursion into speculation, Davy concluded lecture seven with a reaffirmation of the proper use of hypotheses 'as instruments for comparing facts and for ascertaining their minute relations'. When properly used 'they promote in the highest degree the efforts of inventive genius and tend to impress on the understanding the true and unperverted images of nature'. Apparently Davy did not view the Deluge as hypothetical.

In the eighth lecture on mineral metallic veins Davy provided mostly 'insulated facts' derived from mining lore about their directions, and compositions. But these he avers, can hardly be said to belong to a science of geology whose great end is to develop some general principles of reasoning or some simple methods of classing the phenomena so as to guide us by analogy to new truths or to useful applications. But, he goes on, nothing 'is more obscure than the theory of the causes of their formation and of the laws of their changes'. He followed with summary accounts of the speculations of several writers from Agricola to Henckel, relating only the opinions 'of celebrated men, [but] all that they serve to prove perhaps is that when celebrated men amuse themselves with dreaming, they do it almost to as little purpose as common men'.

The explanation of the origins of metallic veins by Werner and by Hutton he finds no more satisfactory than those of earlier writers. It is not an impossible topic for rational inquiry, but we need more knowledge and the better application of chemistry to mineralogy before we can hope for significant success. Meanwhile, Davy stated in conclusion, there is sufficient challenge for the ambition of men of experimental genius 'perhaps for ages'. ⌊Lect. 8⌋

Volcanoes was the last major topic in these lectures. Since at this time he had not seen an active volcano, Davy depended upon the writings of earlier observers of Mt. Aetna and Mt. Vesuvius for descriptions of their activity. These long passages were followed by an extended discussion of previous speculations on the source of volcanic heat. Of the several described, Davy clearly preferred one of the combination of pyrite and pit coal. The pyrite in the proper state of division will spontaneously take fire and in turn ignite the pit coal which, by this hypothesis, would then provide the great heat necessary to melt the adjacent rocks and form the lava. After cautioning the audience against placing 'any indiscrete confidence in the speculations given', Davy justified their presentation by saying that his 'principle object ... was to develop the general facts ... in a connected and analogical order, and to point out the probable relations of their effects to certain known causes'. We ought not to be discouraged by the difficulties in gaining a 'perfect explanation' of volcanic action, however concealed beneath the surface 'that great laboratory of nature' may be. Past difficulties in the understanding of nature have been overcome. 'And the investigation of natural causes is always a happy exercise for the human understanding; not a gratification of idle curiosity, but of the love of useful knowledge. And the development of truths of this kind is of the highest interest, displaying at the same time the talents of man, the majesty and variety of nature, the wisdom and perfection of the laws of nature'. ⟦Lect. 10⟧

In the last half of the final lecture Davy returned to the theme of providential design. Volcanoes may seem accidental, but when accurately considered they will be shown to contribute importantly to the general economy of things that 'they bear a distinct subserviency to the general harmonious series of natural operations'. Most obvious among these contributions is the formation of fertile soils from volcanic lavas. This led him into a general discussion of the formation of soils from other kinds of rocks. He concluded:

> It would be an endless task to detail all the operations by which the beautiful cycle of terrestrial events is preserved in an uniform order. The arrangements of matter are constantly altered; its essence continues inalterable. Amidst the

> various infinitely diversified changes of things nothing can be said to be accidental or without design. Even the most terrible of the ministrations of nature in their ultimate operation are pregnant with blessings and with benefits. Beauty and harmony are made to result from apparent confusion, and all the laws of the material world are ultimately subservient to the preservation of life and the promotion of happiness. /Lect.10/

The themes delineated in these lectures from early in Davy's career are characteristic of his later ones as well. Indeed many passages show a clearer conception of them and a more urgent sense of their importance. Davy's own intellectual excitement underlies his lectures still. The theme of intellectual progress only implicit in the lectures of 1805 becomes distinctly expressed and the contribution of hypotheses to that progress becomes precise even while his distrust of theoretical speculation never wavers.

> Nature is inexhaustible; her objects are boundless. As we can imagine no termination to space, so we can imagine no limit to the combinations and application of matter. Ages may roll on; one theory may succeed another; for these are mutable and

> partake of the nature of the being by whom they are invented; but facts are eternal; the progression of truth even arises from the destruction of hypotheses...[12]

And again in the same year, 1811.

> Nothing is so fatal to the progress of the human mind as to suppose that our views of science are ultimate; that there are no mysteries in nature; that our triumphs are complete, and that there are no new worlds to conquer.
>
> . . .
>
> /Scheele_/ made use of hypothesis only as a guide to investigation; and he formed and relinquished his opinions in the truly philosophical spirit, making them, as it were, the machinery for propelling forwards science, - the mere points for employing the lever of experiment.[13]

Though Davy ceased lecturing at the Royal Institution after 1812, he later found opportunity for the public expression of these same ideas as President of the Royal Society. In his first Presidential Discourse given in December of 1820, Davy combined all three themes in one relatively brief paragraph.

> [I] trust that our philosophers will attach no importance to hypotheses, except as leading to the research after facts so as to be able to discard or adopt them at pleasure, treating them rather as parts of the scaffolding of the building of science, than as belonging either to its foundations, materials, or ornaments; that they will look, where it be possible, to practical applications in science, not, however, forgetting the dignity of their pursuit, the noblest end of which is, to exalt the powers of the human mind, and to increase the sphere of intellectual enjoyment, by enlarging our views of nature, and of the power, wisdom, and goodness of the Author of nature.[14]

The theme of intellectual progress so evident in Davy's public lectures was given cosmic dimensions in his last literary work written during the introspective period of his final illness. In the first dialogue of his posthumously published Consolations in Travel,[15] Davy drew on the eighteenth century traditions of the plurality of worlds and the great chain of being for the frame for an ultimate conjoining of all immortal souls with God, the infinite Intelligence. Life is everywhere in the universe, the spiritual essences, like the material bodies they inhabit, are infinitely varied; they are indeed 'parts more or less inferior of the infinite mind'.[16] Each of these souls or monads, as he variously called them, carried with it from one material embodiment to another, 'only the love of knowledge or of intellectual power, which is ... in its most perfect development ... the love of God'.[17] Each is in a probationary state, its reward or punishment determined by how it has used its intellectual power. When its intelligence has been nobly applied in increasing the knowledge of the world and applying it benevolently, and 'in developing and admiring the laws of eternal Intelligence',[18] the monad will be rewarded by possessing in its next embodiment a greater capacity to receive sensory impressions, and perhaps to dwell on a more intellectually stimulating planet such as Saturn with its rings and many moons. But if the intellectual power is used vaingloriously, or in idle curiosity, 'the being is degraded, it sinks in the scale of existence ...'.[19] But ultimately all the life in the universe must rise through all the forms of beings 'before the consummation of things'.[20]

The dialogue form in which Davy wrote this final work effectively disguises how literally he intended its particulars. But in the <u>Consolations</u> as in the lectures of earlier, happier years, the central value of the intellect is undeniable, both in the moral obligation for its right use and in the consequent rewards. But for all the self-conscious earnestness of the Consolations Davy never expressed his own feelings more effectively than in a lecture of 1809.

> I hardly know which we ought most to rejoice at - the progress that has been made in natural knowledge, or the progress that is to be made. If a limit could be obtained, if we could rest satisfied with what is known, how great a source of activity, profit, and pleasure, would be destroyed! And we cannot be too grateful for that wonderful constitution of the external universe, by which it is rendered an inexhaustible source of interest to the inexhaustible human mind; by which it is so admirably adapted to keep awake that happy curiosity, which is a constant germ of improvement; that noble kind of ambition which continually tends to exalt the intellectual being; that flame of life, unquenchable even in the fountain of knowledge.[21]

Surely we must recognize with Thomas Poole that indeed Davy's 'delight was in his intellectual being'.

NOTES

1. In a letter to Davy's first biographer, John Ayrton Paris, quoted in *Fragmentary Remains*, pp.319-320.
2. Edmund Davy, who witnessed the event, related the account of it to John Davy, who recorded it in his *Memoirs*, vol.1, p.384.
3. Paris, *Life*; citations are to the 1831 single volume edition, p.89.
4. The words are those of Thomas Bernard, as given by H. Bence Jones, *The Royal Institution: its Founder and its First Professors*, London, 1871, p.258.
5. See George A. Foote, 'Sir Humphry Davy and his Audiences at the Royal Institution', *Isis*, 43 (1952), 6-12.
6. Louis Simond, *Journal of a Tour and Residence in Great Britain during the Years 1810 and 1811*, 2 vols., Edinburgh, 1815, vol.2, pp.150-152.
7. The words are those of Sir Charles Elliot, the first Earl of Minto, as quoted by Foote, loc.cit. (5), 10.
8. Fom a lecture of 1811. *Works*, vol.8, pp.354-355.
9. For a brief discussion of the geological content of these lectures and of Davy's geological activities, see Robert Siegfried and R.H. Dott, Jr., 'Humphry Davy as Geologist', *British Journal for the History of Science*,

9 (1976), 219-227.
10. These lectures have been edited for publication, by Robert Siegfried and R.H. Dott, Jr. Since no pagination is available, citation will be made only in the text to the lecture number. In the R.I. Davy Ms, lectures 1-6 are found in Box 16, and 7-10 in Box 17.
11. <u>Works</u>, vol.8, p.183.
12. Ibid., p.321.
13. Ibid., p.318.
14. Ibid., vol.7, p.14.
15. H. Davy, <u>Consolations in Travel, or the Last Days of a Philosopher</u>, 1st ed., London, 1830. The work went through a number of English editions and several translations. All references here are to vol.9 of <u>Works</u>.
16. Ibid., p.239.
17. Ibid., p.247.
18. Ibid., p.248.
19. Ibid., p.247.
20. Ibid., p.245.
21. Works, vol.8, p.351.

Davy's Salmonia

David Knight

Far and away Davy's most successful works were his Agricultural Chemistry, and the dialogues which he wrote when labouring under tedious and ultimately fatal illness: Salmonia, published anonymously in 1828, and Consolations in Travel, which appeared posthumously in 1830. Morris Berman has explained the popularity of the Agricultural Chemistry, based as it was upon lectures delivered before improving landowners at the Royal Institution when it could be thought of as the Society of Husbandry in Albemarle Street.[1] The popularity of the dialogues is perhaps not so easy to account for, especially as they went on selling for the best part of half a century; thus surviving into a world very different from that in which Davy had made his way. An unkind review of Salmonia[2] remarked that it seemed 'a patch-work composed of shreds of anniversary speeches before the Royal Society, articles in Philosophical Journals, and lectures on Natural History to Mechanical Institutions'; and no doubt in an era when mind was on the march such a mixture of information, edification and entertainment by the most eminent natural philosopher of his day formed a most acceptable kind of popular science.

The same critic, John Wilson - with Lockhart, the main support of the obstreperous and fiercely-Tory <u>Blackwood's Edinburgh Magazine</u> - remarked that in angling, Davy was more than an amateur; that indeed he did it well, for a gentleman. The tone of the book is certainly gentlemanly throughout; Davy confined himself to fly fishing for salmon and trout, and treated scientific investigations as something that will interest men of leisure in search of hobbies and subjects of conversation. This after all was the spirit in which in 1823, he recruited Murchison to science:[3] 'I fell in with Sir Humphry Davy, and experienced much gratification in his lively illustrations of great physical truths. As we shot partridges together in the morning, I perceived that a man might pursue philosophy without abandoning field-sports'. Shooting, especially snipe, was Davy's other relaxation, as impeccably gentlemanly as fly fishing, and there are digressions about it in <u>Salmonia</u>. We have come a long way from the professional science upon which Davy founded his career, and from the fundamental work in the laboratory for which he has chiefly been remembered in our century, though perhaps fishing might be regarded as applied natural history.

In his Eloge of Davy, Cuvier[4] referred to
Salmonia and remarked that the many curious observations would make it always an important work in
ichthyology; but he added that science must regret
that so powerful a genius had had to pursue such
distractions and forget chemistry in an attempt to
save his tottering health. Such insignificant
occupations as fishing were necessary to one whose
accelerated career had prematurely brought on the
infirmities of age. While Cuvier should have been
a good authority in determining what was important
in ichthyology, he was perhaps here being generous;
certainly in the standard work on British Fishes of
the 1830s, by William Yarrell, Salmonia hardly
features except for a reference to Davy's observations on the grayling as 'a good history'.

Davy appears to have read writings of Bloch and
of Lacépède on fishes,[5] and these were the standard
works down to those by Cuvier and Agassiz; and
when in 1824 there was a Select Committee set up by
Parliament on the Salmon Fisheries of the United
Kingdom, Davy delivered a brief paper on May 8th
which was published as an appendix to the committee's
report. He proposed three objectives: that more
fish should be allowed to spawn, of all ages and
sizes; that fish should not be killed in rivers
after spawning; and that fry or young fish should
not be killed. To realize these objectives, he
proposed that there should be further restrictions
on netting, a prohibition of fishing at night with

lights, and a longer close season. He referred to Jacobi's experiments, reported in Bloch, which showed that salmon's eggs only hatch in running water saturated with air; but there is really little science in his report. Rather, as in his <u>Agricultural Chemistry</u>, he was happy when he could give a chemical rationalization of what farmers by informal experiment had shown to be the best practice, so here he was using the prestige of science in support of common-sense proposals.

In the <u>Gleanings of Natural History</u>, 1834, of Edward Jesse,[6] an amateur of the subject, we find mention of Davy's <u>Salmonia</u> in a discussion of the generation and habits of eels, which was a live issue in contemporary ichthyology; and Jesse quotes a passage on the swallow where Davy used 'language almost poetical'. He ended his book with another 'poetical' quotation about a page long, because it expressed 'the gratification I have derived in viewing what is beautiful in nature - my pleasant walks by some clear and lively stream, and my strolls through woodland scenery'. Such happy hours 'passed in contemplating the works of a beneficent Creator' should be looked upon 'as neither mis-spent nor unprofitable'. These are reactions which Davy would no doubt have welcomed.

Anyone, on the other hand, coming to his book in search of fishing tips would have been rather disappointed. We learn much more about how fish were actually caught, and we also get a much stronger feeling of a passion for fishing, in William Scrope's <u>Days and Nights of Salmon Fishing on the Tweed</u> of 1843,[7] which was like Davy's and Jesse's books published by John Murray. Scrope was the father-in-law of Poulett Scrope, the geologist, who took his name; and was, like Davy, a friend of Walter Scott. Scrope also manages to be rather wittier; Davy has a somewhat ponderous discussion of the ethics of fishing, urging that fish feel little or no pain when hooked. Scrope argues that he simply makes an imitation fly which an aggressive fish then attempts to murder, thus wantonly intruding himself on the hook in his lawless endeavour to deprive the fisherman of his fly.

One does not then find in <u>Salmonia</u> either a work of serious natural history - and like Yarrell's these could in Davy's time be discursive and even anecdotal - or a manual for the fly-fisherman. Perhaps it might be taken as a work of literature; indeed the references to poetry in relation to Davy's writings made by Cuvier, by Jesse, and others including Scott indicate that the book was so received by some readers. One who found it wanting as literature was John Wilson, in his review in <u>Blackwood's</u>.[8] <u>Salmonia</u> appeared anonymously, but no effort seems to have been made to keep its authorship a secret; Wilson's review begins: 'This is a book on a very delightful subject, by a very distinguished man. But although it is occasionally rather a pleasant book than otherwise, it is not by any means worthy either of the subject or the man - the one being Angling, and the other Sir Humphry Davy'. Scott, reviewing it enthusiastically in the Quarterly, remarked that 'we are indebted to the most illustrious and successful investigator of inductive philosophy which this age has produced', which at the time would have been universally recognised as a circumlocution for Davy.

    Wilson continued his review with some gusto; the Preface declared that Salmonia had been written during some months of severe and dangerous illness, but it struck the reviewer that the author must have been comatose while writing and that his recovery must have been miraculous. Wilson was an expert writer of comic dialogue, famous for his episodes involving the Ettrick Shepherd, originally modelled upon James Hogg but soon acquiring a life of his own. He criticised Salmonia as 'stupid': the dialogue is 'drawling', the interlocutors are 'introduced without dramatic skill', and they have no character - one never knows who is speaking. One of them is called Poietes, and Wilson had been appalled to hear that this poor prosy person was modelled on Wordsworth; another is called Ornither, and yet when there was discussion about eagles he said nothing! We are never told how the four named persons got to their various exotic places, or what they did when they were not fishing; and they seem to be such an 'Exclusive Angling Club' that no fifth

person could join in and make their society less
boring. What some readers found poetical were for
Wilson mere purple passages, attempts at fine
writing, 'sad common-place stuff - very very trashy
indeed'. At one point a large fish was caught and
was to be sent to a prince; here Davy's Whig and
Aristocratic views had led him into writing a
fairy tale. Some of the anecdotes of natural history
also failed to convince Wilson of anything except
the author's ignorance; and as a good Scotsman, he
waxed indignant at patronising remarks about Sabbath
observance.

Wilson was said to be robust but not malicious
in his writing, and that is certainly the way he
seems to have handled Salmonia. He is quite right
that the reader can never tell who is speaking;
and those who sought to find consistently real people in the characters must have had a hard time.
The sentiments expressed are sometimes those associated with Davy's friends; but really all the
characters cannot be other than Davy himself wearing various rather transparent masks. We read the
book not as we might read a novel, to meet interesting fictional characters, but to meet Davy himself
in his leisure moments. As a genuinely anonymous
work, Salmonia might well be found rather dull
and of interest only to the specialist in fly-fishing literature, or sub-literature; but as an
opportunity to encounter one of the great men of
his day, and an important figure in the history of

science, it should not be sneezed at. And after all, John Davy tells us[9] of Davy's companions in fishing and shooting that 'they, indeed, I will now say, were almost his only true friends who were his associates in these sports', and that even if ill 'there he recovered the hilarity natural to his disposition, and appeared in his true character, most cheerful, amiable, and entertaining, and the delight of his friends'.

Walter Scott, in his review of <u>Salmonia</u>, treated it thus, as the informal work of a great man.[10] Scott and Davy had known each other for many years, and Lady Davy was a cousin of Scott's; it was at her request that he undertook the review. 'When great men condescend to trifle', he began in the grand manner, 'they desire that those who witness their frolics should have some kindred sympathy with the subject which these regard'. Fishing is after all the male equivalent of needle-work or knitting, half-business and half-idleness; but in a work by the leading natural philosopher of the day 'we are led to discover the sage even in his lightest amusements'. Where Wilson had deplored taking the antiquated, Cockney, and stiff <u>Compleat Angler</u> as a model, Scott saw this as very proper and was pleased that Davy went beyond Walton in describing fly fishing - the gentlemenly rather than the vulgar pursuit - and in his geographical and social range. To Scott, the tone of the dialogue with its references to the

Creator who has planted a religious instinct in man was just 'what a great and good man's mind might be expected to exhibit' on slow recovery from severe illness; and in his remarks on natural history, he noted Davy's wariness in drawing general conclusions, and his avoidance of dogmatic scepticism - the latter reference is to certain remarks on omens, which could be associated with Davy's reputed superstitiousness. Scott concluded with the fear that over-fishing, and the excessive draining of the country, would soon exterminate the salmon, and that future generations would read Salmonia as we read of the chase of deer, wild boars, or wild cattle.

Davy was pleased with the reception of Salmonia,[11] writing to his wife that 'it has almost rekindled my love of praise'; the terms that Scott used in his review, poet, philosopher, and sage were in fact just those which Davy had used of himself in a rhapsody of uncertain date: 'Oh most magnificent and noble Nature! Have I not worshipped thee ... As Poet, as Philosopher, as Sage?'

An important episode in Salmonia[12] was something about which Davy had also written a poem, in about 1821; the party saw an eagle fishing on a Highland loch, and one of them described how he had seen a pair of eagles teaching their young to fly. For Scott, this scene united the sublimity of Salvator Rosa to the accuracy of Gilbert White;

whereas for Wilson it perpetrated ornithological blunders, for the kind of eagle named would not fish as Davy said it did, dropping from a height into the water. Davy described the bird (Poietes used the word 'animal' to the indignation of Wilson) as 'the gray or silver eagle', and distinguished it from the osprey; it seems probable that it was the white-tailed or cinereous (ashen-grey) eagle, <u>Haliaëtus albicilla</u>, now only seen as a vagrant in Scotland but in Davy's time not uncommon there. A modern ornithological author describes the bird fishing almost as Davy did. In <u>Salmonia</u>, the story of the old eagles teaching the young ones to fly upwards into the sun is told in a straightforward manner; but in the poem Davy used it as a metaphor:

> The mighty birds still upward rose,
> In slow but constant and most steady flight,
> The young ones following; and they would pause,
> As if to teach them how to bear the light,
> And keep the solar glory full in sight.
> So went they on, till from excess of pain,
> I could no longer bear the scorching rays;
> And when I looked again they were not seen,
> Lost in the glory of the solar blaze.
> Their memory left a type and a desire;
> So should I wish towards the light to rise,
> Instructing younger spirits to aspire
> Where I could never reach among the skies,
> And joy below to see them lifted higher,
> Seeking the light of purest glory's prize.

> So would I look on splendour's brightest day
> With an undazzled eye, and steadily
> Soar upwards full in the immortal ray,
> Through the blue depths of the unbounded sky,
> Pourtraying wisdom's boundless purity.
> Before me still a lingering ray appears,
> But broken and prismatic, seen thro' tears,
> The light and joy of immortality.

The passage is important in <u>Salmonia</u> because <u>Haliaëtus</u> is derived from the poetical Greek form of Halieus, a fisherman; and the name of the leader of the fishing party, or Exclusive Angling Club, is Halieus, 'who is supposed to be an accomplished fly fisher', and who, like the parent eagles, is instructing the others. They are: Ornither, a gentleman fond of field sports; Poietes, an enthusiastic lover of nature - both these being less experienced anglers than Halieus; and Physicus, a person fond of inquiries in natural history and philosophy, but a novice in fishing. Apart from their different expertise in fishing, all the characters fit Davy himself: the President of the Royal Society encouraging younger spirits to surpass even his achievements; the keen shooter of partridges and snipe; the poet who loved nature as never mortal man before had done; and the inquirer into natural history and philosophy. It is no wonder that we cannot tell who is speaking when they get off fishing techniques, where Halieus is clearly the expert.

Davy himself wrote[13] that 'these personages are of course imaginary, though the sentiments attributed to them, the Author may sometimes have gained from recollections of real conversations with friends, from whose society much of the happiness of his early life has been derived'; and no doubt those who knew him derived some amusement from identifying who might have said what. In the last dialogue, the ninth day of fishing, we are given a clue that 'a likeness... will not fail to be recognised to that of the character of a most estimable Physician, ardently loved by his friends, and esteemed and venerated by the public'; this was William Babington, to whom Salmonia was dedicated 'in remembrance of some delightful days passed in his society, and in gratitude for an uninterrupted friendship of a quarter of a century'. John Davy warned against identifying Halieus elsewhere with Babington, and also refers to Davy describing his own state of mind and sentiment 'in the character of Physicus' at the end of the book; but Physicus, a man of science taking up fishing in middle age in the first two dialogues, was probably originally based upon Wollaston, as is implied in a note. Indeed the fourth edition of Salmonia, 1851, which has Davy's name on the title-page, has a composite portrait of Davy, Babington, and Wollaston on page 1, as well as notes by John Davy.

At one place Halieus must represent either Babington, or Davy, describing his symptoms as those of a friend. Wilson seized upon an old-maidish passage where Halieus forbids the ordering of another bottle of claret:[14] 'A half pint of wine for young men in perfect health is enough, and you will be able to take your exercise better, and feel better for this abstinence. How few people calculate upon the effects of constantly renewed fever, in our luxurious system of living in England!' The consequence of too rich living was the 'the heart is made to act too powerfully, the blood is thrown upon the nobler parts', finishing up in the head. Free livers must expect, especially if they are in the habit of wading while fishing or shooting, to be killed off by apoplexy or made miserable by palsy; and 'free livers' were those who consumed 'as much animal food as they could eat, with a pint or perhaps a bottle of wine per day'. There are indeed some old men who have both drunk and waded freely, but they are '<u>devil's decoys</u> to the unwary, and ten suffer for one that escapes'.

Halieus then continues, in what must be an oblique reference to Davy, 'I could quote to you an instance from this very county, in one of the strongest men I have ever known. He was not intemperate, but he lived luxuriously, and waded as a salmon fisher for many years in this very river; but before he was fifty (Davy was forty-nine), palsy deprived him of the use of his limbs and he is still a living example of the system which you are ambitious of adopting'. He then produced a maxim which sounds as though it was made up by a nanny, but he attributes it to Boerhaave: 'Keep the feet warm, the head cool, and the body open'. Davy's condition was not as bad as this might imply; but the diagnosis had been that too much blood was going to the head,[15] and after his first attack - which seems to have been a stroke - he was recommended to eat a lot of meat. When this did not work, he was put onto an abstemious regimen, with bleeding prescribed; in his travels into Italy to escape the English winter, he took leeches with him which became frozen solid on the journey, but when thawed were apparently as voracious as ever.

When in Rome at his fiftieth birthday he heard of Wollaston's illness and impending death, writing to his brother on December 21st:[16] 'Poor Dr. Wollaston has had an attack of paralysis, and I am sorry to hear is without hopes. His severe and ascetic life has not preserved him. This complaint is certainly becoming more common in England. I have heard of two or three other friends who have likewise suffered, - spare, abstemious men; James Macdonald is one of them'. Those in the habit of attending funerals will detect the familiar note of triumph of the survivor, especially when it might have been expected that he would be the one to go first. To Jane Davy, he wrote of Wollaston in a similar vein: 'He at least has not suffered from indulgence. I cannot help thinking that a certain quantity of nervous or vital power is given to man, which, when consumed, cannot be replaced, and which limits the period of activity and existence'.

Not only had Wollaston taken great care of his health, but he had built up a fortune from his science, by a process for making platinum; this was something of which Davy disapproved, having a gentlemanly rather than a professional attitude to his science, and refusing to patent his inventions. Davy wrote to his wife:[17] 'It was not worth his while to have died so rich; but I suppose there is pleasure in accumulating. So will W. die! with perhaps two or three hundred thousand; yet these men might have applied money to the noblest purposes. You speak of his malady being a family one. This likewise is my case: my grandfather and six or seven of my great uncles died of apoplexy'. So, from attributing his disease to over-indulgence in drinking, eating and wading in Salmonia, Davy had come to see it either as the consequence of burning up his capital of nervous energy in his pursuit of science, or of hereditary predisposition - both of which are morally unobjectionable!

Salmonia sold fast, and a second edition came out in 1829. Davy wrote of it to his brother:[18] 'I have made the second edition twice as large, and I hope twice as amusing. It contains many of my philosophical views, and some new and I hope true opinions in natural history. I send the copy for the second edition to Murray by the next opportunity'. At the Royal Institution, there is an annotated copy of the first edition, with Davy's amendments written in. To say that the book became twice as large is an exaggeration; it had 335 pages as against 273. Many of the changes are minor, involving a change of a word; and some of the excessive commas characteristic of Davy's style (the result, no doubt, of punctuating for reading aloud) are deleted. There is not much change to the specifically fishy parts of the dialogues, although a large section on the habits of the <u>hucho</u> is added, presumably because Davy had in the interim done a great deal of fishing for these in Austria.

The purple patch with which the book concludes, where Physicus says that he would give all that he has gained in an 'active and not unprofitable life' to recover the freshness of mind he had at twenty-five, was made a good deal purpler for the second edition.[19] The passage now, with references to 'the dew of the dawning morning', 'the great of other ages and of distant places', and the laurel and the oak 'which appeared to offer themselves as wreaths to adorn my throbbing brow', seems to call out for declamation, and is good of its kind though one can never imagine anybody saying it in a conversation between friends. A passage on Everard Home's dissection of an eel, which he supposed to be hermaphrodite, said bluntly 'this circumstance demands confirmation'; this was changed to the more courtly 'I hope this great comparative anatomist will be able to confirm his views by new dissections, and some chemical researches upon the nature of the fringes and the supposed melt'. Davy did not really hope this at all, disagreeing with Home's view; and as John Davy pointed out in the 1851 edition, Davy had been right, and Home wrong. Davy and Home had been earlier associated, with Babington, Brodie, and others; but Home seems to have lost Davy's respect by 1823, when he wrote to John Davy: 'Sir Everard has published his Lectures - a magnificent book as to engravings, chiefly in consequence of the liberality of the Royal Society: and it contains certainly a great mass of valuable matter, with much loose speculation and <u>microscopic</u> physiology'. Babbage later attacked the Royal Society's 'liberality' in this case, in his <u>Decline of Science</u> of 1830.

<u>Salmonia</u> was illustrated with plates, newly engraved for the second edition but omitted from the fourth, where some woodcuts replace them.[20] One of the engravings shows the eagles, surprisingly low down in the foreground; the others are picturesque views of the rivers mentioned in the text. It also has small wood-engravings of fish, scattered through the text. According to Dr. Paris, Davy's first biographer, Lady Davy told him that these were from drawings by Davy himself; and this seems likely, for although John Davy does not mention it, he does refer to his brother's skill in drawing geological features in a landscape, and to his journals with 'figures drawn with pen or pencil of any forms, especially of fish, which were new and interesting to him'. The cuts are attractive; they face either

way, where the usual convention in works of science is that they point to the right. In the annotated copy, the second wood-cut of the grayling has an amendment made to the tail, which is made more sharply forked; and this seems to have been carried out in subsequent editions.

The biggest changes were in the general discussions, where much was added. Davy wrote to his friend Thomas Poole, the tanner of Nether Stowey whom he had got to know in his Clifton days and at whose house he had written Salmonia:[21] 'a second edition will soon be out, which will be in every respect more worthy of your perusal, being, I think, twice (not saying much for it) as entertaining and philosophical'. If we are to meet Davy through Salmonia, it is no doubt the revised version that we should use. In looking within the fisherman for the philosopher, we should not entirely forget the exterior; with his 'curious and elaborate' tackle, his broad-brimmed white hat garnished with flies, breeches with knee-caps made from an old hat, and jacket with numerous pockets - an outfit, as his brother remarks, 'not unoriginal and considerably picturesque'. He was apparently a very successful fisherman; Scott said that Salmonia failed to indicate the inequality between anglers, and Davy was famous for some of his good catches; a salmon of forty-two pounds caught in the Tweed, for example, and not mentioned in Salmonia. He was not always successful; John Davy mentions fishing with him from dawn to dusk in June without raising a fish.

The dialogues begin in London, with a discussion of the ethics of fishing; this includes anecdotes of fish being caught very soon after breaking a line, and therefore probably not feeling any great pain from a hook. The party then assemble for their first day's actual fishing at Denham, on the Colne in Buckinghamshire. This day, unlike any of the others, is dated: 'May, 1810', when Davy was at the peak of his chemical work.[22] John Davy wrote of this period, that 'when his pursuits did not keep him in town, he often made short visits to friends residing in the neighbourhood of London, or went to some trout stream, of which there are so many good ones within twenty or thirty miles of the metropolis, and breathed the fresh air by the river side, and enjoyed the country and his favourite exercise and amusement of fishing together'. The passage in <u>Salmonia</u> describes such a visit, with fishing in the afternoon, in the evening (after dinner at five), and on the following morning. Denham was the seat of Sir George Bowyer, M.P. for Malmesbury and then for Abingdon, whose family had held the property for two centuries, but who sold it in 1813.

A fair amount of informal entomology is taught in the dialogues, as on other days (later there is a reference to Kirby and Spence's immortal tomes);[23] and there is a considerable discussion, not in the first edition, on development and inheritance, with references to Erasmus Darwin, to Buffon, and to Hartley. Of the three, Hartley is praised for his 'profound ideas', the other two being speculative, unsound, and given to wild fancies. Having thus dissociated himself from materialism, Davy then proposes a theory of the inheritance of acquired characteristics, using evidence from domestic selection, including horses, merino sheep, poultry, and domestic pigeons, and goes on to apply this notion to the different kinds of trout - suggesting that cross-breeding commonly takes place even between different supposed species. This does not show that Davy might have written the <u>Origin of Species</u> had he been spared for a few more years, but only that no-one with a professional interest in agriculture and a leisure interest in ichthyology could avoid such questions.

The dialogue is also of interest because it mentions trade secrets being purchased;[26] but in general we are not, in <u>Salmonia</u>, in the world of the Industrial Revolution, except when towards the end we find the happy and religious Austrian peasants contrasted with the idle and conceited lower classes of England, who have had education forced upon them (by some of Davy's patrons, such as Sir Thomas Bernard, if truth is to be told), and have then been made 'tumultuous subjects of <u>King Press</u>, whom I consider as the most capricious, depraved, and unprincipled tyrant, that ever existed in England'. Poietes, who says this, is supposed to be a Roman Catholic; and it is one of the features of Davy's travels that they seem to have made him surprisingly sympathetic towards this Church. He was delighted when Catholic Emancipation was carried, writing to Lady Davy 'I have always considered this point as essential to the welfare of England as a great country, and connected with her glory as a liberal, philosophical, and Christian country'. His travels, on the other hand, did not lead him to overcome his prejudices against the French, characteristic of his generation.

The next dialogue is set on Loch Maree, where the incident of the eagles took place; Davy had been there in 1821, fishing and then on August 12th shooting grouse on the moors of Sir George Mackenzie, well known for his interests in chemistry, geology and agriculture.[25] As well as fishing, and advice on the cooking of salmon, we find remarks on Sunday observance, and the introduction of a poacher, which give some local colour to the dialogue. There is also an interesting discussion of the process of dying, added after the first edition; where the peaceful deaths of Cullen, Black and Blagden are described, and suffocation is said to be rather agreeable than otherwise, from Davy's own experiments with gases at Clifton, and from the suicide of the younger Berthollet.

Also in Scotland, we find a discussion of

instinct; this was a topic about which Kirby and Spence had had a good deal to say, and over which they were not in agreement.[26] Davy considered that instincts might be referred to the immediate impulse of God, but seems to have preferred to think of them as the result of general laws governing the universe. He did not believe with Paley that there was a good analogy between the world and a machine, seeing organisms and machines as essentially different because the former embodied a principle of conservation as well as perfection. Men having reason did not need ordinary instincts but Davy believed that man was possessed of a religious instinct, leading to natural religion which when guided by revelation could produce that most 'pleasurable state of the human mind ... when, with intense belief, it looks forward to another world and to a better state of existence, or is absorbed in the adoration of the supreme and eternal Intelligence'. In rejecting Paley's argument from the watch, Davy urged the inscrutability of God, 'the one incomprehensible Cause of all being'; in this as in his chemistry, he was in reaction against the received opinions of the late eighteenth century.

The next place where the anglers meet is at Downton, near Ludlow, the home of Thomas Andrew Knight, the plant physiologist and a friend of Davy's for many years, who supplied notes for the third edition of the <u>Agricultural Chemistry</u>, and to whom the fourth edition was dedicated.[27] Davy wrote that Knight's researches were 'not merely curious, but useful'. The house had been laid out by Richard Payne Knight, the aesthete and brother of the horticulturalist, in the picturesque manner of which he was a pioneer; Davy had fished there frequently with friends, and when Knight's son was killed in a shooting-accident in 1828, Davy was himself desolated and wrote a letter of condolence. Knight's daughters wrote of Davy's death, that there was no-one in whose society their father 'so delighted, and whom he could so ill at this time have spared; there were many points in which the feelings of both were peculiarly in accordance'. Davy left Knight 'a seal ring, bearing the impression of a fish, in remembrance of the days passed together on the banks of the Teme'.

Here the grayling is the fish they are after, and the general discussion is about the reproduction of eels. There is then more entomology, and a discussion with illustrations of artificial flies drawn by the side of those they are meant to imitate. This conversation again turns to religion, with the insect as the type of man, rising from his crysalis-coffin to a new and higher life, and the happiness of death under the vision of celestial glory and the pure and intense love of God. When the party find themselves later in Austria, it is about the design and wisdom evident in the correlation of the parts of creatures that they talk; this principle, made much of by Cuvier, enabled one to reject stories of mermaids or krakens, and contained all that was of any value in the doctrines of phrenology. Davy took a less sceptical view of omens and superstitions:[28] 'The deep philosopher sees chains of causes and effects so wonderfully and strangely linked together, that he is usually the last person to decide upon the impossibility of any two series of events being independent of each other'; but he did in fact explain the basis of some superstitions, while feeling unable to account for 'the more mysterious relations of moral events and intellectual natures'.

Davy was one of the first to whom the term 'professional chemist' might be applied, naturally with reservations.[29] He sounds 'modern' in his attitude to politics, being so John Davy tells us 'free from party bias, and who regarded the then perplexing and anxious state of things very much in the light of a problem to be solved' - a man of science coming to the support of the existing order of things. He seems 'modern' too in his rootlessness; cut off from his family and home by his meteoric rise, he rarely revisited Cornwall and seems to have been as happy in Austria or Italy as in England. Apparently sociable and easy with friends when fishing, he seems to have got along for months abroad without any of his fellow-countrymen; indeed the diaries he drew upon for parts of the convivial Salmonia were written on solitary trips.

Outside this circle of old friends, most of them met through his work, he may have hoped for love but all he got, like modern man, was recognition. He longed to be the eagle teaching its young to fly ever upwards, but he had no children, was essentially a lone rather than a team worker, and managed to spoil his relationship with Faraday - who was of course like him in these respects. One might have expected that his last visits to the Continent, under the shadow of death, would have been exceedingly gloomy; but this is not the impression that one gets from Salmonia or Consolations, or from the letters written during these years. Fishing and religious reflections, the composition of these books of dialogues, his own company and that of a few foreigners, seem to have sustained him very well - the works of God rather than those of man were what gave him real pleasure, marking him out as a Romantic. In Salmonia we do not seem to meet the chemist who modified everybody's notions of affinity, elementary status, and acidity; but we do see almost all other aspects of the man, and some of them in a light otherwise unobtainable.

NOTES

1. M. Berman, Social Change and Scientific Organization: The Royal Institution, 1799-1844, London and Ithaca, 1978. On Davy's Consolations, see my paper 'The Scientist as Sage', Studies in Romanticism, 6 (1967), 65-88. On the general background of science in Britain about 1830, see S.F. Cannon, Science in Culture, New York, 1978.
2. Blackwood's Edinburgh Magazine, 24 (1828), 248-272. The names of the reviewers are to be found in W.E. Houghton et al, Wellesley Index to Victorian Periodicals, 2 vols., Toronto, 1966-72.
3. A. Giekie, Life of Sir R.I. Murchison, 2 vols., London, 1875, vol.1, p.94. On chemistry as a profession, and Davy as an early professional, see C.A. Russell et al, Chemists by Profession, London, 1977, pp.24-26.
4. G. Cuvier, Eloges historiques, Paris, n.d., p.355. W. Yarrell, British Fishes, London, 1836, pp.80-82.
5. [H. Davy], Salmonia, 3rd ed. London, 1832, pp.233, 227. Parliamentary Papers, VIII, Reports from Committees, IV, London, 1824, pp.144-145. See my paper, 'Agriculture and Chemistry in Britain around 1800', Annals of Science, 33 (1976), 187-196.

6. E. Jesse, Gleanings of Natural History, 2nd series, London, 1834, pp.65, 85, 320f. On Jesse, see D.N.B.
7. W. Scrope, Days and Nights of Salmon Fishing in the Tweed, London, 1843, reprint Edinburgh, 1975, p.82. The publisher was John Murray II, who was like Davy born in 1778. On Scrope, see D.N.B.
8. See note (2). Scott's review is in The Quarterly Review, 38 (1828), 503-535. On Wilson and his journalism, see D.N.B.
9. Memoirs, vol.2, p.287.
10. Scott, loc.cit. (8).
11. Fragmentary Remains, pp.303, 14.
12. H. Davy, Salmonia, 1832, pp.98f.: A. Rutgers in Gould's Birds of Europe, London, 1966, p.17; Memoirs, vol.2, p.157 and compare vol.1, p.377.
13. H. Davy, Salmonia, 1832, p.vii. J. Davy, Preface to 4th ed. of Salmonia, London, 1851, and Memoirs, vol.2, p.303. Babington had interests outside medicine: see W. Campbell Smith,'Early mineralogy in Great Britain and Ireland', Bull. Br.Mus.Nat.Hist. (hist.Ser.), 6 (1978), 49-74, pp.59f. In the same volume of the same journal pp.75-108, there is an account of Davy's friend and later protégé, J.G. Children, by A.E. Gunther. Whatever one thinks of Davy's philosophical views, it is of interest to note that as one might expect of one whom Cuvier described (op.cit.4) as a dying Plato, organised his

fishing book as an ennead; there is some discussion of Neoplatonism, Naturphilosophie, and materialism with reference to Davy, in my Transcendental Part of Chemistry, Folkestone, 1978, chap.3.

14. H. Davy, Salmonia, 1832, p.125; Wilson, loc. cit. (2), pp.267f.
15. Memoirs, vol.2, p.220; Fragmentary Remains, pp.275, 280.
16. Memoirs, vol.2, p.336; Fragmentary Remains, p.307.
17. Fragmentary Remains, p.310.
18. Memoirs, vol.2, p.332.
19. H. Davy, Salmonia, London, 1828, p.271; 1832 ed., p.325. The reference to Home is on the previous page; see Fragmentary Remains, p.242. C. Babbage, Reflections on the decline of science in England, London, 1830, pp.103f.
20. The first edition has only the woodcuts of fish, and the entomological plates. The second and third have engravings by Edward Finden of the scenes of the dialogues. The eagle facing p.95 seems to be after Bewick's white-tailed eagle, his first study for British Birds (reproduced in C.E. Jackson, Wood engravings of Birds, London, 1978, p.41) reversed. The edition of Salmonia in vol.9 of the Works contains only entomological plates. The cut of the grayling is on p.175 of the first ed., and p.212 of the third. On editions, see J.Z. Fullmer,

Sir Humphry Davy's Published Works, Cambridge, Mass., 1969, p.97. Paris, *Life*, single volume edition 1831, p.457; *Fragmentary Remains*, pp. 15, 302. Introduction, p.14, by G.S. Myers to R.L. Playfair and A.C.L.G. Gunther, *The Fishes of Zanzibar*, Kentfield, California, 1971, on the way fish usually face.

21. *Memoirs*, vol.2, pp.340, 286f; Yarrell, op.cit. (4), vol.2, p.20; Scott, loc.cit. (8).
22. On Bowyer, see *The Victoria County History, Buckinghamshire*, London, 1925, vol.3, pp.255f; F. Boase, *Modern English Biography*, London, 1892, vol.1, column 363. *Memoirs*, vol.1, p.263.
23. H. Davy, *Salmonia*, 1832, p.242; W. Kirby and W. Spence, *An Introduction to Entomology*, 4 vols., London, 1815-26. The evolutionary speculations come in *Salmonia*, pp.73f.
24. H. Davy, *Salmonia*, 1832, pp.91, 290f. On trade and science, see D.F.S. Scott, *Luke Howard, 1772-1864*, York, 1976, p.4. *Memoirs*, vol.1, p.272; vol.2, pp.374f; *Fragmentary Remains*, pp.284, 292f, 311f.
25. *Fragmentary Remains*, pp.237f; on Mackenzie, see *D.N.B.* On the younger Berthollet, see M. Sadoun-Goupil, *Le chimiste C.L. Berthollet, 1748-1822*, Paris, 1977, pp.68-71; *Salmonia*, 1832, p.114f.
26. H. Davy, *Salmonia*, 1832, pp.160f. W. Kirby, *Bridgewater Treatise*, ed. T.R. Jones, 2 vols., London, 1853, vol.2, pp.162f. For a modern

discussion of men, machines, and organisms, see W.H. Thorpe, <u>Purpose in a World of Chance</u>, Oxford, 1978, chap.2. See also <u>Memoirs</u>, vol.2, pp.89f.

27. H. Davy, <u>Salmonia</u>, 1832, p.237. T.A. Knight, <u>Physiological and Horticultural Papers</u>, London, 1841, pp.46-49; cf. <u>Fragmentary Remains</u>, p.287, where Davy tried to arrange a marriage for young Knight.

28. H. Davy, <u>Salmonia</u>, 1832, p.197; cf. <u>Memoirs</u>, vol.1, p.149.

29. See note (3); Berman, op.cit. (1); <u>Memoirs</u>, vol.2, p.88. We even see the founder of the London Zoo in <u>Salmonia</u>, 1832, p.313.

A Note on Humphry Davy's Experiments on the Respiration of Nitrous Oxide

E.B. Smith

In 1772 Joseph Priestley discovered nitrous oxide, or nitrous phosoxyd or gaseous oxyd of azote as it was first known. The properties of the gas attracted considerable interest and were the subject of much speculation. Dr. Samuel Latham Mitchill advanced the view that nitrous oxide was the 'oxide of septon' which when breathed or applied to the skin even in minute quantities, had the power of carrying disease (qv. Neve, pp.13-17). Davy's knowledge of this theory led to his first experiments with the gas in his attic bedroom in the spring of 1798, when he was apprentice to the surgeon-apothecary, John Bingham Borlase of Penzance:

> The fallacy of this theory was soon demonstrated, by a few coarse experiments made on small quantities of the gas procured from zinc and diluted nitrous acid. Wounds were exposed to its action, the bodies of animals were immersed in it without injury; and I breathed it

mingled in small quantities with common air, without remarkable effects. An inability to procure it in sufficient quantities, prevented me at this time from pursuing the experiments to any greater extent. I communicated an account of them to Dr. Beddoes.[1]

When Davy joined Beddoes' Pneumatic Institution at Clifton in October 1798,[2] he undertook an extensive investigation of the physiological effects of nitrous oxide and other gases. The results were published in the summer of 1800 as <u>Researches Chemical and Philosophical chiefly concerning Nitrous Oxide or Dephlogisticated Nitrous Air, and Its Respiration</u>. His note-books at the time said 'the researches have been made since April 1799 the period when I first breathed nitrous oxide. Ten months of incessant labour were employed in making them, three months in detailing them'.[3] His first experiments disclosed that breathing the gas was 'attended by a highly pleasurable thrilling, particularly in the chest and the extremities', though 'whenever its operation /breathing/ was carried out to its highest extent... impressions ceased to be perceived... and voluntary power was altogether destroyed so that the mouthpiece generally dropped from my unclosed lips'.[4] Others were induced to try the gas, eighteen of whom described their sensations in contributions to Davy's publication. One of Beddoes' patients said he 'felt like the sound of a harp' on breathing the gas.[5] Coleridge wrote of feeling 'a highly pleasurable sensation of warmth over my whole frame'.[6] Southey wrote to his brother:

> Oh, Tom! Such gas has Davy discovered, the gaseous oxide! Oh, Tom! I have had some; it made me laugh and tingle in every toe and finger tip. Davy has actually invented a new pleasure for which language has no name. Oh Tom! I am going for more this evening; it makes one strong and so happy, so gloriously happy! Oh, excellent air bag! Tom, I am sure the air in heaven must be this wonder-working air of delight.[7]

Davy himself took moonlight walks and tried to emulate his poetic friends by composing verse under the influence of gas:

> Not in the ideal dreams of wild desire
> Have I beheld a rapture-wakening form;
> My bosom burns with no unhallow'd fire,
> Yet is my cheek with rosy blushes warm.[8]

Davy's attitude to animal experiments was more orderly. Writing of the effects of nitrous oxide on warm-blooded animals, he described fourteen experiments on mice, guinea pigs, rabbits, cats, dogs and birds. Of his five principal conclusions, the most important were:

> 1. Warm-blooded animals die in nitrous oxide infinitely sooner than in common air or oxygen; but not nearly in so short a time as in gases incapable of effecting positive changes in the venous blood, or in non-respirable gases.
>
> 2. Peculiar changes are effected in the organs of animals by the respiration of nitrous oxide. In animals destroyed by it, the arterial blood is purple red, the lungs are covered with purple spots, both the hollow and compact muscles are apparently very inirritable, and the brain is dark-coloured.[9]

The first point he established to his satisfaction with three experiments on pairs of carefully matched animals (see Table 1. p.237), observing that time to death in N_2O was over twice that in hydrogen and water. Though these particular experiments were few, the design was good, and he had the results of many other investigations with nitrous oxide and other gases to support his conclusions. The modern interpretation of this result is not that nitrous oxide is capable of supporting life in any positive sense but that anaesthetised animals survive longer in anoxic conditions. The protection from convulsions conferred by the anaesthetic and the lowered metabolic rate are factors which could lead to prolonged survival in the gas. However, the colour changes observed by Davy are not in keeping with modern observations. A possible impurity, nitric oxide, binds strongly to haemoglobin, more strongly in fact than carbon-monoxide. The complex however has a bright red colour and is without the bluish tinge observed with carbon monoxide.

Davy also investigated the effects of nitrous oxide on amphibians, fishes, insects and vegetation. He breathed hydrogen, carbon dioxide, water gas ($CO + H_2$) and nitric oxide - the last two experiences he was lucky to survive. Two of his observations deserve mention. He diluted CO_2 with air and found that it 'stimulated the epiglottis in nearly the same manner as pure carbonic acid'.[10] Second, by careful analysis of expired gas he concluded that 'the exhausted capacity of my lungs was equal to about 41 cubic inches'.[11]

Davy clearly recognised the analgesic properties of nitrous oxide, using it to ease the pain from an erupting wisdom tooth.[12] He wrote in his summary, 'As nitrous oxide in its extensive operation appears capable of destroying physical pain, it may probably be used with advantage during surgical operations in which no great effusion of blood takes place'.[13] How far Davy was interested in the analgesic as opposed to the 'sensational' properties of the gas is not known, and in any case, in 1801, he left Clifton to join the Royal Institution and his research in this subject soon came to an end. The possibility of general anaesthesia was lost to mankind for almost half a century. It was not until 1844 that Horace Wells, an American dentist, used nitrous oxide for the extraction of one of his own teeth. Wells was led to try the gas after attending a popular demonstration by Gardner Quincy Coulton, whose advertisements quoted a letter from Southey to Davy in which he wrote that 'he supposed the atmosphere of the highest of all possible heavens to be composed of this gas'. Within a few years surgical anaesthesia became established practice but the use of nitrous oxide was not without problems. The effective partial pressure required for anaesthetic action is high (see Table 2, p.237), higher than can be admin-istered for any length of time if the oxygen partial pressure is to be adequate. Many of the early surgical applications required very short times of exposure and the danger of anoxia was not great, but by 1868 the dangers of administering nitrous oxide without adequate oxygen were recognised.[15] Controversy then raged on the concentration of oxygen required to strike the proper balance between the risk of cyanosis and too low a level of anaesthesia. Paul Bert attempted to use the gas in pressure chambers to circumvent this difficulty, but not surprisingly the idea did not catch on. Despite these problems, nitrous oxide became established as a dental anaesthetic, as an analgesic in childbirth and as a carrier gas for use with other agents. In the latter role it can contribute a significant fraction of an anaesthetic dose and reduce the amount of more potent, less rapidly eliminated, anaesthetic that needs to be administered.

Table 1. Effects of Nitrous Oxide Compared with those Produced by Immersion in Water and Hydrogen.

Rabbits	2 months old	H_2	dead in 3/4 min.
		N_2O	dead in 2½ mins.
Rabbits	3 months old	H_2	½ min. -recovered
		N_2O	1½ min. -recovered
Kittens	2 months old	H_2O	dead in 2½ mins.
		N_2O	dead in 5¼ mins.

Table 2. Anaesthetic Doses of Nitrous Oxide

Animal	End Point	Date	ED_{50} Partial Pressure of N_2O/atm.
Mouse	Rolling response	1972	1.5
Dog	Surgical anaesthe-tic	1969	1.9
Man	Surgical anaesthe-tic	1967	1.01

Taken from a more extensive summary in K.W. Millar, W.D.M. Paton, E.B. Smith and R.A. Smith 'Physico-chemical approaches to the mode of action of general anaesthetics', Anesthesiology, 36(1972),339.

NOTES

The author wishes to acknowledge the assistance of Dr. S. Daniels and Professor W.D.M. Paton.

1. Works, vol.3, p.269.
2. See T.H. Levere, 'Dr. Thomas Beddoes and the Establishment of his Pneumatic Institution', Notes and Records of the Royal Society. 32 (1977).
3. Works, vol.3, preface.
4. Ibid., pp.272-273
5. Ibid., p.294.
6. Ibid., p.306.
7. Quoted in J. Kendall, Humphry Davy, Pilot of Penzance, London, 1954, p.46.
8. Ibid., pp.46-47
9. Works, vol.3, p.212
10. Ibid., p.281
11. Ibid., p.241
12. Ibid., p.276
13. Ibid., p.329.
14. K. Bryn Thomas, 'Editorial', Anaesthesia, 33 (1978), 903.
15. See Victor Robinson, Victory over Pain, New York, 1946.

POSTSCRIPT

A tribute to Davy, composed by Richard Gendell, was sung by Brenda Wootton for the entertainment of those attending the Bicentenary symposium. A light-hearted tribute, which Samuel Smiles would not have included in his portrait of the self-made hero, but one from which, remembering Davy's conviction of his own genius, he might not have dissented altogether.

HUMPHRY DAVY

Words and Music by Richard Gendell

Chorus: There's lots of things that I can do --
I'm Humphry Davy
And oh, I am a clever boy -- I'm Humphry Davy.

1. Monday I discover things like sodium and chlorine
Mixing up my chemicals the stink is appalling
This is Potassium, found by Davy!

2. Tuesday is the day I make a safety lamp for miners
Let them have it as a gift, they'll never get a finer
This is Magnesium, found by Davy!

3. Wednesdays I go lecturing at the Royal Institution
All the ladies love to watch me making up solutions
This here is Faraday, found by Davy!

4. Thursdays I make laughing gas and sniff it up my 'hooter'
Take a little overdose and nearly end my future
This stuff is strontium, found by Davy!

5. Fridays I go fishing in the rivers and the oceans
Takes a mighty clever fish to 'scape our Davy's notion
This stuff is Barium, found by Davy!

6. Saturday's for travelling in Europe for pleasure
Studying phenomena and fishing at my leisure
This is a medal I got from 'Boney'.

7. Sunday I write poetry and books, you should read them,
Science and philosophy and fishing you should heed them
I'm very clever you know, I'm Davy!

INDEX

Abernethy, John (1764-1831), 18
Admiralty, Board of, 86
Agassiz, L. (1807-73), 203
agricultural interest, 17, 42, 44
Agriculture, Board of, 42, 44
Ampère, A-M. (1775-1836), 104, 132, 138
anaesthesia, 16-17, 235-7
'Annual Anthology', 35
Apreece, Jane, see Davy, Lady

Babbage, C. (1792-1871), 85, 217; 'Decline of Science', 87
Babington, William (1756-1833), 212, 217
baconian science, 44, 49, 52, 154, 185
Banks, Sir Joseph (1743-1820), 51, 59, 78-9, 85
Baring, Sir Francis (1750-1818), 24
Beddoes, Dr. Thomas (1760-1808), 8, 11ff, 44, 61, 62, 232; 'Considerations on Factitious Airs', 16
Bence Jones, Dr. Henry (1813-73), 24
Berkeley, Bishop (1685-1753), 46
Berman, M., xi, 17, 24, 27, 37, 42, 201
Bernard, Sir Thomas (1750-1818), 220
Bert, Paul, 236
Berthollet, C.L. (1748-1822), 97, 102, 109, 114, 115; 'Chemical Statics', 114, 123

Berzelius, J.J. (1779-1848), vii, xi, 33, 48, 110, 123, 126, 127, 136, 151-2
Black, Joseph (1728-99), 70
Bloch, M.E., 203, 204
Boase, Henry (1799-1883), 23
Borlase, John Bingham (1752-1813), 8, 9, 20, 21, 22, 231
Boscovich, R.G. (1711-87), 46
Boulton, Matthew (1728-1809), 11-12
Bowyer, Sir George, M.P., 219
Brande, W.T. (1788-1866), 24, 27, 79
Brentano, Clemens, 46
Bristol, 11-12
British Museum, 86
Brodie, Sir Benjamin, (1783-1862), 217
Brooke, J.H., x
Brougham, Henry (1778-1868), 48
Brown, John (1735-88), 13-14
Buffon, G.L. (1707-88), 220
Burnet, Thomas (1635?-1715), 'Sacred Theory of the Earth', 186-7

Cambridge, medical education at, 8, 26
Carlisle, A. (1748-1840), 66
Caroline, Queen, 85
Cartwright, F.F., 16
Castlereagh, Lord (1769-1822), 86
chemistry (see also Davy, Work on), acids, theories of, x, 106, 114, 121ff; affinity, 68; analysis, 102, 112-13; atomism, 45;

chemistry (cont'd)
Avogadro's hypothesis, 153;
British tradition, 61,
69-70, 96; chemical
'revolution', 18, 87-8, 95,
121; combustion, 62, 76,
122, 142; compounds,
nature of, 65, 67, 71,
126-7, 133-4, 142, 147-9;
conceptualization, 59ff,
73ff, 87-8; dualism, 135-
6, 148, 149-50, 151-2;
dynamical theories, 34,
45-6, 47; electrochemical
theories, 72, 135-6, 149-
54; elements, 45, 48, 71,
145; French theories of,
47, 61, 64, 70, 74, 75,
76, 77, 88, 99, 109-10,
114, 115, 121ff; history
of, ix, 76, 121-2, 123-4;
medical uses, 13, 16, 18,
23, 24-5, 27, 44; nomen-
clature, 62, 132, 139;
ontology, 126, 127-8, 135,
138-9, 142-4, 145; phlogiston theories, 121, 135,
144, 150; Romantic view
of, 34, 45-7
Children, J.G. (1777-1852),
27
Clarke, E.D. (1769-1822), 26
Clayfield, William, 17
Clifton, 11, 18, 19
Clément, N. (1779-1841),
103-5, 132
Colchester, Lord (1757-
1829), 79
Colebrooke, H.T. (1765-1837),
83
Coleridge, S.T. (1772-1834),
33, 34, 38, 41, 43, 45ff,
53, 233

contagion, 13, 15
Cornwall (see also Penzance),
6, 11-12, 21
Coulton, Gardner, Quincy, 236
Crosland, M.P., ix, 127
Cruickshank, W., 73
Cullen, William (1710-90), 13,
221
Cuvier, G. (1769-1832), 142,
203, 205, 224

Dallas, Sir Robert (1756-1824),
78
Darwin, Erasmus (1731-1802),
15, 220
Davy, Edmund (1785-1857), 74
Davy, Humphry (1778-1829),
General:
'Agricultural Chemistry',
201, 204, 222; appointment
to R.I., 17, 25, 43, 69;
apprenticeship, 7, 231;
'Consolations in Travel',
2, 28, 36, 49, 54, 181,
195-7, 201, 225; education,
34; 'Elements of Chemical
Philosophy', 33, 133, 135,
151; election as P.R.S.,
59, 79; work as P.R.S.,
80-87; 'fragmentary'
achievement, vii-viii, 6,
33, 110; honours, 50, 52;
ideas misrepresented, x,
135, 140, 146-9; lectures,
general, 7, 25, 69, 70,
111, 178ff; on agricult-
ural chemistry, 4; Baker-
ian 1st, 72-3, 100, 108;
2nd, 73, 107-8; 3rd, 74-5;
5th, 75-6; 6th, 61; on
geology, 182ff; marriage,
3, 28, 113;

Davy, Humphry
  General (cont'd)
    poems, 34-5, 38-40, 210-11, 233; 'Sons of Genius', 35ff; 'Salmonia', 201ff; reviews of, 201, 202-3, 205-7; skill in drawing, 217; travels to Continent, 3, 95, 104, 225; Ireland, 3-5; Scotland, 7
  Attitude to:
    angling, 202ff; death, 5-6, 221; field-sports, 202, 211; France, 70, 99, 134, 136, 221 (see also France, rivalry with); genius, 35ff; glory, 36ff; health, 203, 213-14, 215; Ireland, 3-5; lower classes, 3, 4, 220; materialism, 5, 134; medical profession, viii, 7, 25-7; nature, 33, 39-41, 114, 211; patenting of inventions, 215; poetry, ix, 35, 40, 42, 52-3; politics, 36, 85, 224; post-mortem examination, 5-6; the Press, 220; progress, 50-1, 178-9, 193-4, 195-6, 197; religion, 222, 223, 225; Roman Catholicism, 3, 221; sabbath observance, 207, 221; scientific discovery, viii, 37, 43, 44, 49, 52-3, 84-5; scientific method, 51, 64; generalisation, 129, 209; use of hypotheses, 33, 46, 107-8, 184, 190, 194, 195; scientific profession, 78, 110, 202; utility, 37, 49, 50-2, 54, 84; wealth, xi, 13, 215; women, 82, 180
  Characteristics:
    ambition, 36, 43, 50; arrogance, 84, 138; boldness, 108; creativity, 177ff; eclecticism, 107, 129, 139; experimental ability, 63-4; individualism, 113; intellectual delight, x, 137, 177ff; lack of discipline, 33, 110-11, 116; love of praise, 2, 43, 50, 51-2, 78, 209; malleability, xi, 44; opportunism, 129; patriotism, xii, 70, 84-5, 137; polemical skill, 139, 141; rootlessness, xii, 224; snobbery, vii, 117, 202; sociability, 208, 212, 223, 224-5; solitariness, 224-5; superstitiousness, 4, 209, 224
  Work on (see also chemistry):
    acids, 102, 122ff; agricultural chemistry, 50, 71, 204; elements, general: 45, 62, 67, 108, 132-3, 145; metallic, 48, 73-5, 100, 101, 122; halogens, 76, 102-5, 122, 140; non-metals, 47, 75, 122; electrochemistry, 45, 47, 66-9, 71ff, 149-52; electrochemical corrosion, 50, 77; flames, nature of, 77; geology, 24, 70, 182ff; heat, nature of, 61-3, 64; iodine, 100, 102-5, 141-2; light, nature of, 61-3; nitrous oxide, 16, 66, 99, 231-5; safety-lamp, 50-2,

244

Davy Humphry
  Work on (cont'd)
  77; 'silex', 64-5;
  tanning, 50, 71;
  voltaic pile, 45, 66-9,
  72ff.
Davy, Lady (1780-1855), née
  Jane Apreece, 3, 85, 208,
  217
Davy, John (1790-1868), 7,
  9, 20, 27, 64, 96, 102,
  105, 116, 208, 212, 219
de Capell Brooke, Arthur, 83
de Luc, J.A. (1727-1817), 187,
  188
Desormes, C.B. (1777-1862),
  104, 132
disease, concepts of, 13-15
dispensaries, 20-21, 27
Dulong, P.L. (1785-1838),
  136-8, 146
Dumas, J.B. (1800-84), 148-9,
  152; 'Leçons de la
  philosophie chimique', 140,
  149
Dunkin, Robert, 9

East India Company, 83
Edinburgh, medical education,
  25
Edwards, Dr. E.C., 21
Edwards, John, 23
empiricism, 41
entomology, 219, 223
evolution, 220

Faraday, Michael (1791-1866),
  225
Ferriar, Dr. John (1761-1815),
  63
Forbes, John (1787-1861), 22
  23

Fordyce, George (1736-1802), 8
France (see also chemistry,
  French theories), 42, 47,
  95ff; rivalry, ix, 70, 95,
  99ff, 129ff; scientific
  community, 96, 98, 104,
  109-12
Fullmer, J.Z., ix, xi, 141, 142

Gay-Lussac, J.L. (1778-1850),
  ix, 96ff, 124, 130, 131, 133,
  134, 138, 139-40, 146-7, 152,
  155
geology:
  Biblical correspondence, 186;
  of Cornwall, 21, 23; history
  of geological thought, 183-
  8; metallic veins, 184,
  190-1; primitive rocks, 183,
  188-9; providential design,
  182, 186, 187-8, 192-3;
  secondary rocks, 183, 189-90;
  uses of, 182; volcanoes,
  184, 191-2
George III, 85
George IV, 85
Gerhardt, C.F. (1816-56), 125,
  149, 153, 154-5
Gilbert/Giddy, Davies (1767-
  1839), 11, 64, 85, 178
government support of science,
  81, 84-6
Graham, Thomas (1805-69), 152
Gregory, William (1803-58),
  128, 136, 155-6
Griffin, J.J. (1802-77), 149

Hartig, Arthur, 83
Hartley, David (1705-57), 40,
  41, 220
Hartley, Sir Harold, 122

Harwood, Busick (1745?-1814), 8
history, xii, 1-2, 76-7, 122; whig interpretations, 125, 128
Home, Everard (1756-1832), 216-7
Hooke, Robert (1635-1703), 185
Hornblower, J.C. (1753-1815), 12
Hutton, James (1726-97), 185-6, 190

ichthyology, 203ff, 216-17
idealism, 41
ideology of science, 37, 42, 44
infirmaries, 21, 22
inheritance of acquired characteristics, 220
instinct, 222

Jesse, Edward (1780-1868), 'Gleanings of Natural History', 204, 205
Jesus College, Cambridge, 7, 26

Kant, I. (1724-1804), 41
Keats, J. (1795-1821), 2
King, John (1766-1846), 8, 17-19, 43
Kinglake, R. (1865-1842), 17
Kirwan, R. (1733-1812), 187
Knight, David, xi, xii, 134
Knight, Richard Payne (1750-1824), 223
Knight, Thomas Andrew (1759-1838), 222-3

Lacépède, Comte B.G. de, 203
Laënnec, R.T.H. (1781-1826), 23
Laurent, A. (1808-53), 122, 154, 155
Lavoisier, A. (1743-94), 76, 88, 113, 115, 121ff; table of elements, 45, 47, 61-2, 64 (see also chemistry: conceptualization, and French theories)
Leibniz, G.W. (1646-1716), 'Protogaea', 187, 189
Levere, T.H., viii, x .
Liebig, J. (1803-73), 122, 148, 149
literature, 205
Liverpool, Lord (1770-1828), 86
Locke, John (1632-1704), 40, 41
London Institution, 24
Longitude, Board of, 86
Lunar Society, 11
Lyell, Charles (1797-1875), 1

Mackenzie, Sir George (1780-1848), 221
Malta, university, 27
Malthus, Rev. T.R. (1766-1834), 26
Mayhew, Henry (1812-1887), 'The Wonders of Science', 10
'Medical Repository', 14, 15
medicine, 6-9, 12ff
Mitchill, S.L. (1764-1831), 13-15, 231
mineralogy, 21, 24, 191
Murchison, Sir R.I. (1792-1871), 202
Murray, John II (1778-1843), 205

natural history, 205, 207, 209
Neve, M., viii, xii,
Nicholson's 'Dictionary', 61
Nicholson's 'Journal', 66, 67, 68, 72
nonconformists, 81-2
Nottingham infirmary, 20

ornithology, 210
Ostwald, W. (1853-1932), 'Classics of Science', 105, 115
Otter, William (1768-1840), 26

Paris, J.A. (1785-1856), 9, 20, 21-22, 103, 104, 217; biography of HD, 22; 'Guide to Mount's Bay', 22; 'Philosophy in Sport..', 23
Pearce, William, 26
Peel, Sir Robert (1788-1850), 86
Penneck, Henry (1762-1834), 8, 23
Penzance, 7, 10-11, 20-23; Public Dispensary & Humane Society, 20-23
Playfair, John (1748-1819), 52
Pneumatic Institution (see also Beddoes), 8, 17, 232-3
Pool, P.A.S., 20
Poole, Thomas (1765-1837), 177, 218
Priestley, Joseph (1733-1804), 13, 46, 231
professional science, 110, 202, 224
professional status, 77-8
provincial culture, 11, 20, 22

reform, ix, 59ff, 80ff
Risse, Günter, 13
Ritter, J.W. (1776-1810), 46
romanticism, 2, 38, 41, 112, 114, 225
Romantic poets (see also individual names), 36, 39, 52
Royal Geological Society of Cornwall, 20, 21
Royal Institution, 17, 24, 28, 37, 42, 44, 70, 96, 110, 178-9, 201
royal medals, 86
Royal Society, 42, 51, 59, 78-86, 96, 194, 217
Royal Society of Literature, 86
Royal Zoological Society, 86
Rumford, Count Benjamin (1753-1814), 24, 44
Rush, Benjamin (1745-1813), 15

Salmon Fisheries, Select Committee 1824, 203-4
Schelling, 'Naturphilosophie', 41, 45-6
scientific community, 77ff, 98ff
scientific societies, 80, 87
Scott, Walter (1771-1832), 38, 205, 206, 208-9, 218
Scrope, William (1772-1852), 'Days and Nights of Salmon Fishing..', 205
Scrope, G.J. Poulett (1797-1876), 205
Shuckburgh, Sir Francis, 83-4
Siegfried, R., x, 126, 144
Simond, Louis, 179
Smiles, Samuel (1812-1904), 'Self-Help', 52

Southey, Robert (1774-1843), 35, 38, 233
Stahl, G.E. (1660-1734), 61

Thenard, L.J. (1777-1857), 101, 102, 103
Thomson, Thomas (1773-1852), 125
Tonkin, John (1719-1801), 9, 10
trade secrets, 220
Truro hospital, 21

Walton, I., 'Compleat Angler', 208
Watt, Gregory, 12
Watt, James (1736-1819), 11-12
Wells, Horace, 236
Werner, A.G. (1749-1817), 185-6, 190
Whiston, William (1667-1752), 189
Whitehurst, J. (1713-88), 187
Wilson, John (1785-1854), 202, 205-7, 210
Winchelsea, Earl of, 83
Wollaston, W.H. (1766-1828), 212, 214-5
Wordsworth, William (1770-1850), 34, 38, 40, 113, 206

Yarrell, William (1784-1856), 'British Fishes', 203, 205
Young, Thomas (1773-1829), 26